D1566452

flies for
Steelhead

BY DICK STEWART & FARROW ALLEN

Book Design and Illustrations • Larry Largay
Photography • Dick Stewart

Published by Northland Press, Inc.
P.O. Box 280
Intervale, NH 03845
USA

Distributed by Lyons & Burford
31 West 21 Street
New York, NY 10010
USA

© February 1992 by Northland Press, Inc.
All rights reserved

Printed in the United States of America by Capital Offset Company

First Edition

ISBN 0-936644-08-7 Hardcover
ISBN 0-936644-09-5 Softcover

PREFACE

Steelhead. The mere mention of the word conjures up images of Pacific rainforests and strong, streamlined, bright silver fish urged from the cold ocean currents and battling upstream into mighty rivers like the Columbia, then to more intimate and picturesque tributaries, ever driving inland, ever restless, awaiting their time to spawn. These steelhead "trout," commonly regarded as anadromous strains of the rainbow trout, are considered to be close cousins of the Pacific salmon. Some anglers prefer to confine the title of steelhead to sea-run forms which persist in their native habitat. Following the successful introduction of transplanted stock into the Great Lakes, the definition of steelhead has come to include all migratory rainbows, whether anadromous or lake run.

Compared to trout and Atlantic-salmon fly fishing, with its roots in British sporting tradition, fly fishing for steelhead is a recent development, beginning near the turn of the century, concurrent with the westward expansion to the Pacific coasts of both the United States and Canada. The techniques and tackle used for Atlantic-salmon and trout were carried west. In the 1890s, western fly-fishing activity was centered in San Francisco. Anglers fished locally in the San Leandro River, San Mateo and Bay Creeks for trout, salmon and steelhead with snelled wet flies they'd brought from the east. As transportation improved, fishermen traveled north and discovered the bounty of the Eel River. These inquisitive anglers helped establish Eureka as an angling center and made lasting contributions to the development of steelhead fishing.

The first fly-fishing shop opened in Grants Pass, Oregon, near the banks of the Rogue River and became the headquarters for steelhead fishing in southern Oregon. It was here that the unique Rogue River style of tying flies and fishing from boats developed over the next 40 years. In central Oregon, steelhead fly fishing centered around the Forest Service camps on the North Umpqua River.

In Washington, during the mid 1930s, a collection of individual fly tiers and fishermen together with several angling clubs from the Seattle area attempted to have Deer Creek and and a portion of the North Fork of the Stillaguamish River set aside for "fly fishing only." It took these devoted sportsmen nearly ten years to achieve their goal but they never gave in and their efforts exemplify the spirit of northern Washington's steelhead community.

Further north, much of British Columbia was inaccessable except for the southern region around Vancouver Island. Following World War I, access gradually improved into southern British Columbia, but it wasn't until the late 1940s and 1950s that most of the province was penetrated by steelhead anglers. During the same time frame Alaska, too, became accessible to the traveling angler.

Between 1875 and 1900, steelhead eggs from California, Oregon and Washington were being shipped east. Smolts, fingerlings and fry were stocked in various American and Canadian tributaries of the Lakes Michigan, Ontario, Huron, Superior and Erie. By the 1920s, steelhead were established in the Great Lakes and many of their tributaries, providing a significant sport and profitable commercial fishery, but unregulated commercial fishing and lamprey eel predation almost wiped out these stocks. In the mid 1950s a successful lampricide treatment was developed, and by the mid 1960s these parasites were brought under control. Commercial fishing was abolished and additional stocks of steelhead were planted. The steelhead fishery was back in full swing.

While western flies generally adhere to the form and character of Atlantic-salmon patterns, most of the Great Lake's steelhead-fly patterns seem remarkably uninfluenced by traditional Atlantic-salmon flies. There are, of course, many exceptions. Midwestern patterns often resemble trout-fly imitations of local nymphs or natural spawn (although some look outlandish enough to hang on a Christmas tree).

Accordingly, the style of fishing matches the style of the fly. It is not surprising to find that many midwestern steelheaders fish like "trout fishermen," casting upstream, presenting the fly dead drift in a natural way, while west-coast anglers tend to cast down-and-across stream, swimming a fly through the pool as an Atlantic-salmon angler might do.

We present here a wide variety of flies, originating from different geographies, and revealing a diversity of styles. We have tried to organize these patterns into categories that are clear and make sense to the reader and fly tier. In some instances the flies are not easily categorized, so we have exercised our best judgement and trust that it helps you in using this book.

Our intent is to present a pattern book of contemporary flies that are in actual use, and being fished in steelhead rivers across North America. To help compose this list we contacted steelhead guides, fly tiers, writers, anglers and reputable fly-fishing shops throughout the United States and Canada. Whenever possible the flies have been tied by their originators, or tiers who are familiar with the originals. Many of the flies pictured are of exhibition quality, and look like they belong in a frame - not at the end of a leader. This is because we encountered many fly tiers throughout the U.S. and Canada who tie all their flies to the highest standard. Many steelhead tiers study 19th-century classic Atlantic-salmon-fly tying and apply the disciplines to their own creations. They fish with these beautiful flies and readily admit that although the steelhead probably don't care, they do. It's part of the romance of both fly tying and steelheading; it's in keeping with silk flosses, natural feathers, misty rivers and silvery fish.

In presenting the dressings of the photographed flies, we omitted, for the most part, any reference to hook style or type. This is due to a lack of consensus among both tiers and anglers. We leave it to individual tiers to select the hook that best meets their needs. Most flies have been tied on traditional Atlantic-salmon hooks, notably several models from Partridge, particularly the Bartleet range; as well as the Alec Jackson Spey Hook and other black loop-eye models. Similarly, we have made little reference to hook size because the choice is usually determined by water conditions, the season, local preferences and such.

Since most flies are dressed with black heads, for the sake of simplicity we have only indicated head color when it deviates from this standard black.

The identification of some of the modern synthetic materials poses a real problem in the preparation of a book of this sort. We often encountered identical, or very similar, materials being sold under two or three or more brand names. Whenever possible, we specify what we believe to be an understandable generic name so the fly tier will find it easier to locate materials with the same properties.

We are experienced fly tiers and between us have fished for steelhead on the west coast in Washington and Oregon and in a number of rivers of the Great Lakes. Although we contacted as many steelheaders as possible in order to develop a complete and representative range of patterns, we concede our limitations. If significant patterns and fly tiers have been overlooked, the fault is entirely ours.

This book would not have been possible without the help of others. Particularly we would like to thank the individual fly tiers and fly-fishing shop personnel who willingly answered our endless questions and provided us with original flies, up-to-date histories and background information. We are especially indebted to Marty Sherman, Editor of *Flyfishing* magazine, for providing us with access to many important contacts; Alec Jackson, for coordinating our efforts in Washington; and Frank Lendzion for organizing many of the important fly tiers from Michigan. Others who deserve special mention are John Shewey, Dave Hall, Joe Howell, Bill McMillan and Kent Bulfinch. Nor would this book be possible but for the enormous pioneering contributions of Trey Combs, whose knowledge and understanding is reflected through his important writings on steelhead.

On the practical side we offer our thanks to Jack Russell, Editor of *American Angler,* for his editorial advice; Fran Stuart for editorial assistance; Larry Largay for art and design, and Bob Stewart for his technical expertise in putting the 320 color photographs onto printed pages.

CONTENTS

Tied by John Newbury

AIR B. C.

Tail:	White calftail		body hair
Body:	Deer or elk body hair dyed orange, spun and clipped to shape	Wing:	A section of wavy white hair, taken from the tip of a calftail, curling upward and clipped short
Side wings:	Unclipped tufts of the orange		

The Air B.C. began in 1981 as one of Bill McMillan's experimental Bombers, but when it raised only one fish it was unceremoniously retired for the season. The following year McMillan gave his only example to British Columbia anglers Jim Abbott and Don Collis who found it to be an effective pattern on the Dean River. The fly became an established producer of steelhead and they named it after the Canadian airline which uses the same colors: orange and white.

Tied by Dick Stewart

BOMBER, PURPLE

Tail:	Moose body hair colored in a dye bath of mixed purple and fluorescent pink dyes		forward
		Body:	Purple moose body hair spun and trimmed to shape
Wing:	Same hair as tail, flared and set		

This version of the Purple Bomber was designed by British Columbia guide Bob Clay for the Kispiox River. Although Clay readily admits that he wasn't the first to tie a purple Bomber, most of the ones he'd seen before were tied with deer and not moose-body hair, and none had his distinctive fanned wing which causes the fly to wake erratically. As in this example, steelhead Bombers are often tied without a palmered body hackle.

Tied by Scott Ripley

BOXCAR

Tag:	Flat silver tinsel	Wing:	White bucktail or calftail
Tail:	Red hackle barbs	Hackle:	Brown, heavily dressed
Body:	Peacock herl		

This pattern was originated by Wes Drain of Seattle, who pioneered the use of dry flies for steelhead in Washington state during the late 1940s. The Boxcar remains popular today and is in common use by dry-fly fishermen.

Tied by Bill Logan

BUCKTAIL CADDIS

Tail:	Golden pheasant tippet barbs		with an extra turn or two taken at the throat
Body:	Yellow or orange chenille		
Hackle:	Palmered brown, tied in by the tip,	Wing:	Natural brown bucktail

When used with a floating line, this simple fly - which is quite buoyant due to its bucktail wing and palmered hackle - can be fished either just below the surface or in the surface film. If a deep presentation is desired, the Bucktail Caddis is effective fished on a sinking line.

BULKLEY MOOSE

Tail: Dark moose body hair
Body: Butt end of tail fibers brought forward and tied down (optionally the front ⅔ of the body may be dubbed with fur for a buggy look)

Wing: Large bunch of moose body hair
Head: Divide the flared butts of the wing and saturate with thick rubber cement (Pliobond) and trim

John Murtz of the Fish'n Factory in Smithers, British Columbia, developed the Bulkley Moose in the late 1980s for the Bulkley River. Cast downstream and permitted to swing across the current, the Moose, because of its stiff head, imparts a lot of action to tempt a steelhead.

Tied by Farrow Allen

BULKLEY MOUSE

Tail: Natural deer, moose or elk body hair, tied short, not extending beyond the hook barb
Body: Butt ends of the hair used for the tail bound to the hook with criss-

cross wraps of thread
Wing: Natural deer, moose or elk body hair
Head: Flared hair from the wing, clipped to form a head

The Bulkley River is a tributary of British Columbia's Skeena River, and is ideal water for skating a dry fly in either slick or broken water. The Bulkley Mouse was developed by a British Columbia guide, Collin Schadrech, during the late 1970s and early 1980s. It is considered the most effective type of dry-fly pattern for that river. When dressed with an underwing of pearlescent Flashabou it is known as a Disco Mouse (which see).

Tied by Kelvin McKay

CADDIS FLASH

Tail: Orange crystal flash
Body: Burnt orange crystal chenille
Throat: Orange crystal flash
Wing: Dark brown deer body hair, spun

on to form the wing with the majority of hair ending up on top. The clipped butt ends form the head

A waking dry fly developed by John Shewey and Dave McNeese in 1987 for the Deschutes River where steelhead are often lured by surface presentations. To improve flotability, Shewey suggests treating the crystal chenille with fly floatant before applying it and wrapping it as tightly as possible.

Tied by John Shewey

CIGAR BUTT

Tail: White calftail
Body: Natural deer body hair, spun and clipped to look like a discarded

White Owl Panatela
Wing: White calftail
Throat: Stiff moose hair (optional)

This variation of the standard Atlantic-salmon Bomber was designed by Keith Stonebreaker of Lewistown, Idaho, during the late 1970s for dry-fly fishing on the Clearwater River. By eliminating the hackle, the Cigar Butt - which is most effective tied on small hooks, down to size 8 or 10 - plows through the water rather than skating on it.

Tied by Dick Stewart

Tied by John Shewey

Tied by Kaufmann's Streamborn

Tied by Bill Bakke

Tied by Randy Stetzer

COAL CAR DAMP

Tail:	Dark brown fitch tail	Rib:	Fine gold wire
Tag:	Flat gold tinsel	Wing:	Divided dark brown fitch tail tied forward
Body:	Rear ¼: orange floss		
	Next ¼: dark red floss	Throat:	Claret or black crystal flash
	Front ½: black seal fur or substitute	Collar:	Long, soft black hackle
		Head:	Claret

This fly was developed in 1986 by John Shewey based on an earlier wet fly of Randall Kaufmann's - the Coal Car (which see). This is a true "damp" fly - one that fishes in the surface film, producing a subtle wake that will often take a fish that has swirled at a dry-skating pattern but not taken it.

DISCO MOUSE

Tail:	Dark deer or moose body hair	Wing:	About a dozen strands of pearl Flashabou over which is deer or moose body hair, flared and clipped to form a head that is flat on top
Body:	Butt ends of the hair used to make the tail bound to the hook shank with criss-cross wraps of the tying thread		

A variation of the Bulkley Mouse originally tied by Bulkley River guide Collin Schadrech. Its popularity has extended into California and Alaska.

DRAGON FLY

Tail:	Deer body hair		The hair is divided to extend at right angles from each side of the hook shank
Body:	Orange to yellow-orange dubbing or yarn		
Wing:	Deer body hair tied on with the butt ends toward the eye of the hook and the tips pointing back.	Head:	The butt ends of the wing hair are secured on top and clipped at an angle, causing the fly to skate

The Dragon Fly was inspired by the Atlantic-salmon fly, Ingalls' Butterfly. It was originated in the late 1960s by Bill Bakke, Director for Resource Conservation of Oregon Trout. Trey Combs, writing in *Steelhead Fly Fishing and Flies* described the Dragon Fly as "... one of the best half-dozen summer steelhead flies around . . . Fished damp it wobbles, churns and paddles to create mini-wakes that alarm steelhead into striking."

FLUTTERING TERMITE

Tail:	Red squirrel tail	Wing:	Very stiff black moose or similar straight black hair, divided and set forward
Body:	Blend of orange poly yarn and fluorescent orange seal fur or substitute		
		Hackle:	Dark dun saddle

The "Termite" was originated for Washington's Washougal River by Randy Stetzer, a well-known Deschutes River guide, fly tier and fly fisherman from Portland, Oregon. It is intended to imitate the erratic behavior of the large carpenter ants that hatch each autumn in great numbers, then fall clumsily into the rivers, struggling and fluttering as they attempt to become airborn.

FOAM STONE

Body:	Orange closed-cell foam, tied in segments with orange thread
Wing:	Light elk hair
Head and collar:	Elk hair dyed brown tied to form a bullet head and collar
Note:	The rear three segments of the foam body are pre-formed on a

straight pin using a ⅛" piece of foam that is folded in half, top and bottom. This is removed from the pin and slipped onto the hook (as though you were baiting the hook with a worm) and the final segments are formed on the hook

Joe Howell of the Blue Heron Fly Shop in Idleyld Park, Oregon, introduced this pattern for trout in the mid 1980s. Fished dead drift, Howell describes it as an "unsinkable killer trout fly." In large sizes, and fished the same way, it accounts for many steelhead as well.

Tied by Joe Howell

GIANT STONE SKATER

Tag:	Oval gold tinsel
Tail:	Orange crystal flash
Body:	Rear half: Burnt orange seal fur or substitute
	Front half: Brown seal fur or substitute
Beard:	Orange crystal flash
Wing:	Red squirrel tail
Head and collar:	Dark deer hair spun and clipped in the style of a Muddler Minnow

John Shewey, who originated this fly for Oregon's Deschutes River in 1988, has grown to consider it more of a waking fly than a skating one. As such, it is a productive searching pattern. He writes "If a steelhead rises more than once without taking this fly. . . switch to a smaller darker pattern . . ."

Tied by John Shewey

GREASE LINER

Tail:	Fine chestnut color deer body hair
Body:	Dark grayish tan to black fur, or whatever dark dubbing matches the color of local egg-laying adult caddisflies
Throat:	A sparse beard of grizzly hackle
Wing:	Dark deer body hair extending only to the end of the dubbing, clipped to leave a tuft of butt ends. (optionally lacquered)

This important pattern was created in 1962 on the Wenatchee River by one of the northwest's best-known steelhead anglers, Harry Lemire of Black Diamond, Washington. Lemire's own words describe the Grease Liner simply as "a waking fly of unquestionable merit." Usually tied on a light-wire hook, it was designed for low-water angling after observing that steelhead seemed more inclined to take a floating fly dragging across the surface than one drifting naturally with the current.

Tied by Harry Lemire

HALLOWEEN CADDIS

Tail:	Speckled partridge fibers
Butt:	Red-orange seal fur or substitute
Body:	Golden-olive seal fur or substitute
Rib:	Oval gold tinsel
Throat:	Red Antron, brushed out
Wing:	Deer body hair dyed red-brown
Head:	Butt ends of the wing, clipped flat and lacquered
Thread:	Orange

Jim McGeachie, a respected steelhead guide and fly tier from Innerkip, Ontario, originated this fly for fishing the steelhead rivers in northern Michigan. McGeachie began working on this pattern during the fall of 1984 and by 1987 settled on this as the "right" dressing, which is effective in riffles and tailouts throughout most of the fall.

Tied by Jim McGeachie

Tied by Umpqua Feather Merchants

HUMPY, ORANGE STEELHEAD

Tail:	Natural moose, elk or deer body hair		pulled forward forming a hump
Underbody:	Orange tying thread	Wing:	Moose, elk or deer body hair
Overbody:	Moose, elk or deer body hair	Hackle:	Brown
		Head:	Orange

The Humpy style of dry fly is generally attributed to Jack Horner of San Francisco, who also developed Horner's Silver Shrimp (which see). In recent years steelheaders have become increasingly interested in dry-fly fishing and a variety of traditional dry-fly patterns, dressed in steelhead colors and proportions, have proved effective. Near the top of this list of traditional dry flies is the high-floating Humpy.

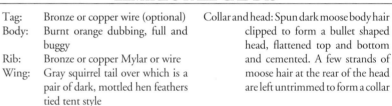

LEMIRE'S FALL CADDIS

Tag:	Bronze or copper wire (optional)	Collar and head: Spun dark moose body hair
Body:	Burnt orange dubbing, full and buggy	clipped to form a bullet shaped head, flattened top and bottom
Rib:	Bronze or copper Mylar or wire	and cemented. A few strands of
Wing:	Gray squirrel tail over which is a pair of dark, mottled hen feathers tied tent style	moose hair at the rear of the head are left untrimmed to form a collar

This fly was first tied in 1984 by Harry Lemire who describes it as a "damp-waking" pattern. Tied in a variety of body colors it is a good imitation for many adult caddisflies. Lemire suggests fishing it with either a riffling hitch or on a greased line with a greased leader.

Tied by Harry Lemire

LEMIRE'S IRRESISTIBLE

Tail:	Fine deer body hair dyed black	Wing:	A single upright tuft of deer body hair dyed black
Body:	Deer body hair dyed black, spun and clipped to shape and trimmed flat on the bottom	Hackle:	Black, trimmed across the bottom

This simple black fly has accounted for many steelhead throughout the northwest including one of over 23 pounds that Lemire beached on the Dean River in 1973. When tying this pattern it is important to trim the body and the hackle flat across the bottom so that the entire fly rests on the surface of the water.

Tied by John Newbury

MOOSE TURD

Tail:	White calftail	Wing:	White calftail, a piece from the kinky tip of the tail, curling up and clipped to ½″ to ¾″
Body:	Black or dark brown deer or elk body hair, spun and clipped		

First tied in 1975 by Bill McMillan, author of *Dry Line Steelhead and Other Subjects*, during a period when he was intensely interested in the effect of different Bomber patterns on steelhead. He observed that the Bomber's traditional palmered hackle added nothing to the appeal of the fly to steelhead, while the curly tips of calftail hair definitely provided the best waking action. Fellow angler Randy Stetzer suggested cutting the wing to help keep the fly from drowning.

OCTOBER CADDIS

Tail: Calftail dyed yellow
Body: Yellowish-orange or fluorescent orange yarn
Wing: Red squirrel tail or calftail, divided and tied pointing forward (tie in before winding the body)
Throat: Sparse brown hackle wound behind the wing

Originated by Bill Bakke, Director for Resource Conservation of Oregon Trout, the popular October Caddis is fished by riffling it in the surface film to imitate a struggling adult caddis. The divided wings are pointed forward to make the fly to wobble erratically when "hitched," presenting a tempting target for steelhead.

Tied by Bill Bakke

POOLDOZER

Tail: Dark coastal deer
Body: Natural caribou body hair, spun and clipped
Wing: Short piece of packaging foam, trimmed into a small triangle, tied extending forward over the eye of the hook
Head and collar: Deer body hair dyed rusty brown, spun rough and untrimmed

The Pooldozer is an easily-tied, hair-body skater originated by Dr. Wes Terasaki of Issaquah, Washington. Its effectiveness as a summer and fall pattern, in either slow or fast water, was brought to our attention by Steve Brocco of the Eastside Anglers in Redmond, Washington. The modern foam materials are certain to play an increasingly-important role in surface-type flies in the future.

Tied by Wes Teraski

RIFFLE DANCER

Hook: Standard black turned-up-eye, bent upward ⅓ way back from eye
Tail: Deer body hair
Abdomen: Butt ends of the tail bound down with tying thread, about ⅔ way up the hook shank
Thorax: Deer body hair, spun and clipped flat on top and allowed to extend ¼″ on the bottom
Wing and head: A large bunch of deer hair tied on top, divided to flare to each side, with the butt ends trimmed to extend just above and beyond the hook eye. On top of these ends a short bunch of moose mane is added to provide more stiffness.

Mark Pinch of Spokane, Washington, designed this fly to skitter, skate and slide across the surface, aggravating a steelhead into striking.

Tied by Dick Stewart

RUSTY BULLET

Body: Fluorescent orange yarn
Head and collar: Bullet style, with collar hair extending to the bend of the hook
Wing: Pair of orange grizzly hackle tips directly behind the bullet head with the stems stripped and left as feelers in front

This bullet-head skater succesfully mimics the abundant Dicosmoecus caddisflies, commonly called "fall caddis" that are indigenous to the coastal rivers of Oregon and Washington. The Rusty Bullet was designed by Joe Howell using tying procedures borrowed from Keith Fulsher's Thunder Creek flies and Bob Borden's more recent Krystal Bullet series.

Tied by Joe Howell

Tied by Joe Howell

SILHOUETTE STONE, LIGHT

Tail:	Light bleached elk hair	Hackle:	Light ginger, tied very full
Body:	Golden yellow yarn or dubbing	Wing:	Light ginger swiss straw, tied at the head and also behind the hackle
Body hackle:	Light ginger, palmered and clipped short	Antennae:	Gray rubber hackle
Underwing:	Light bleached elk, 180 degrees over the top of the body	Head:	Orange thread with black lacquer on the top side

The Dark Silhouette Stone is tied with an orange body and dark hair to imitate the giant western black stonefly while the Light Silhouette Stone resembles the large western golden stonefly. Originated by Joe Howell, it's very effective when steelhead are taking surface presentations.

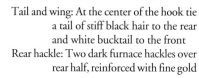

Tied by Joe Rossano

SPEED SKATER, BLACK

Tail and wing:	At the center of the hook tie a tail of stiff black hair to the rear and white bucktail to the front		wire
		Hair hackle:	Spin two opposing bunches of black deer body hair, push together, trim and cement butts
Rear hackle:	Two dark furnace hackles over rear half, reinforced with fine gold		

A skating pattern that really moves fish, this great locator fly can produce some very exciting takes. Inspired by Lee Wulff's Prefontaine Skater, Joe Rossano's Speed Skater is reminiscent of several Atlantic-salmon dry-fly patterns.

Tied by Umpqua Feather Merchants

STEELHEAD BEE

Tail:	Red squirrel tail		vided and cocked forward
Body:	Three equal sections, brown, yellow and brown dubbing, dressed full	Hackle:	Brown, sparse and not too stiff so that the fly will sit in the surface film and not on top of it
Wing:	Red squirrel tail tied upright, di-		

The Steelhead Bee is probably the best-known pattern of Roderick Haig-Brown of Vancouver Island, British Columbia, one of the West's most prolific writers on steelhead. The Bee is often tied with soft hackle and designed for fishing naturally in the film. One of the earliest dry flies that was tied specifically for steelhead fishing, it remains popular.

Tied by Bill McMillan

STEELHEAD CADDIS, McMILLAN

Body:	Pale amber-orange dubbing		body hair, spun and clipped
Wing:	Light mottled turkey wing, folded tent style over the body	Note:	Tied in a variety of body colors including black, olive, yellow and bright orange
Head and collar:	Sparse light colored deer		

Bill McMillan developed this pattern in 1975 ". . . to represent the large-bodied caddisflies that emerge on most northwest rivers . . . during September and October." McMillan writes that "once the temperature of a river reaches 48 degrees or higher . . . surface angling methods will move more steelhead per hour of casting time than any other single level of presentation." It fishes best with a riffling hitch to ensure that it creates a wake on the surface.

STEELHEAD SKATER, GRIZZLY AND PEACOCK

Tail:	Black moose hair tied full, 1½ times the length of the hook shank		fine gold wire
		Body hackle:	Grizzly saddle tied in by the tip, palmered over the body
Wing:	Black moose hair, tied beneath the hook, divided and set forward	Hackle:	Grizzly saddle
Body:	Peacock herl, counter ribbed with		

Bob Wagoner of the Fly Den in Lewiston, Idaho, began developing the idea for this pattern in 1973 in an effort to put the unique floating qualities of moose hair "under the hook where it will float . . . instead of just looking pretty." By the late 1980s the Skater was finalized and was immediately acknowledged as an effective new skating dry fly. It is also tied with brown hackle and peacock, or brown hackle and an orange crystal-flash body.

Tied by Farrow Allen

TELKWA STONE

Tail:	Goose biots, dyed brown, secured on each side of the body	Wing:	Natural elk hair
		Head:	Butt ends of the wing flared up and clipped short. If desired, a wrap of black poly dubbing may be placed in front of the deer hair
Egg sack:	Dark brown dubbing wound at end of the body (optional)		
Body:	Moose body hair lashed with tying thread and extending past the hook bend	Antennae:	Brown goose biots

Mike Maxwell who, with his wife Denise, operates the Gold-N-West Flyfishers shop in Vancouver, British Columbia, originated this pattern. Both are steelhead guides specializing in dry-fly fishing. Maxwell is also an expert instructor in two-handed Spey casting, or Spey fishing as he prefers to call it.

Tied by Mike Maxwell

THOMPSON RIVER RAT

Tail:	Light green bucktail, long	Wing:	Light green bucktail, tied long and on each side of the body
Body:	Natural caribou, spun and clipped		
Hackle:	Grizzly, palmered over the body		

This ungainly looking fly was originated for the Thompson River by Ehor Boyanowsky who previously lived in Nova Scotia where he fished for Atlantic salmon. After moving to Vancouver he was elected president of the Steelhead Society of British Columbia.

Tied by Kelvin McKay

WALLER WAKER

Tail:	Black moose body hair	Beard:	Stiff moose body hair, reaching past the hook point
Body:	Moose or deer body hair, spun and clipped to shape in alternating bands of light and dark colors	Wing:	White calftail, divided and extending forward

This series of skating dry flies was introduced in about 1985 by Lani Waller of Novato, California, while he was working on a series of instructional video tapes for 3M/Scientific Anglers. The Wakers enjoyed a tremendous response from steelhead and steelhead anglers alike. According to Waller, summer-run fish seem to be most inclined to rise to a dry skated or waking fly, but speed is critical and it is better to move the fly too slowly rather than too fast.

Tied by Lani Waller

Nymphs

Tied by Backcast Fly Shop

Tied by Mike Mercer

Tied by Mark Noble

Tied by Kaufmann's Streamborn

BLACK STONE

Hook:	Caddis larva hook	Legs:	Black hackle
Tail:	Black goose biots	Wingcase:	Black duck or goose quill
Body:	Peacock herl		

This dressing was submitted by Steve Forrester of the Backcast Fly Shop in Benzonia, Michigan. It is one of his most popular generic stonefly imitations, and a consistent producer that has been fished with good results on the Platte and Betsie Rivers in both the fall and spring.

BRINDLE BUG

Tail:	Two divided brown hackle tips	Rib:	Fine oval gold tinsel (optional)
Body:	Black and yellow variegated or mixed chenille (the first turn of chenille is taken under the tail to cock it upward)	Collar:	Brown hackle
		Note:	The shank of the hook is often wrapped with lead wire for additional weight

On California's Klamath River they say "if you're not fishing a Brindle Bug, you're not fishing." It is a useful summer and fall pattern on most rivers in northern California and southern Oregon. The Brindle Bug was introduced around 1960 by professional fly tier Lloyd Silvius of Eureka, California, and is often classified as a wet fly rather than a nymph. Two popular variations include the Brindle Bug Nymph of Austin McWithey and the Brindle Bug Rubberlegs.

BURLAP CADDIS

Body:	Natural burlap fibers wound around the shank (may be counter-wrapped with fine gold wire)	Head:	Dubbed black marabou or ostrich herl
Collar:	Ringneck pheasant rump feather	Note:	Often weighted with lead wire

This nymph form was developed by Mark Noble as an offshoot of the popular Burlap wet fly that has been fished in northern California since the mid 1940s. During the winter steelhead are prone to taking nymph imitations fished deep and naturally along the stream bottom. The pattern has become very popular in California and wherever caddisflies are abundant.

CASED CADDIS

Hook:	6x long		the hackle and provide protection for the fragile herl
Body:	Peacock herl over a base of lead wire	Head:	A band of light gray dubbing followed by black dubbing that is well picked out
Hackle:	Brown saddle, palmered and clipped short		
Rib:	Copper wire, helping to bind down		

Steelhead are frequently attracted to the wide range of natural insects they encounter when re-entering their native rivers to spawn. While female steelhead are digging redds in the gravel, many cased caddis become dislodged and are set loose into the current. This imitation of a cased caddis larva should be fished deep and drifted naturally along the stream bottom.

CHIRONOMID

Body: Black angora yarn, mohair or dub-
        bing

Wing: Black Fly Foam shaped as shown

This pattern was designed about 1988 by Jim Rusher, owner of Whitaker's Sport Shop in Pulaski, on the banks of New York's Salmon River. Rusher tied this fly to represent the larger Chironomid midge pupae which are abundant from December to February. He has found large quantities of Chironomids in the stomachs of freshly-killed steelhead at this time of year. The fly-foam wings help keep the fly buoyant and off of the bottom when drifting it deep.

Tied by Jim Rusher

DISCO CADDIS

Body: Light green (or any appropriate
        color) braided Mylar tubing
Thorax: Natural hare's mask dubbing, and

a collar of guard hairs to imitate legs

The Disco Caddis was originated in 1989 by Walt Grau, a successful steelhead guide from northern Michigan. Grau says that the light-green tinsel-body fly is "an effective variation of the Green Rockworm so often fished in Michigan."

Tied by Walt Grau

EARLY DARK STONEFLY

Hook: Size 8 to 14 curved nymph hook
Tail: Mottled brown hen hackle
Abdomen: Brown seal fur substitute
Rib: Copper wire over the abdomen
Thorax: Brown seal fur substitute, picked-

out to simulate legs
Wingcase: Lacquered dark duck or goose
          wing quill, folded to suggest three
          segments

This stonefly nymph was originated by Terry Lyons from Leslie, Michigan, a regional executive director of the Federation of Fly Fishermen. After many years of observing Michigan steelhead's "affinity for stonefly nymphs," Lyons perfected this productive and easily tied imitation. It is best in "rock or cobble stretches" fished dead drift on the bottom.

Tied by Terry Lyons

FILOPLUME HEX

Rear section:
Tail: Gray ostrich barbs
Abdomen: Tan-amber dubbing
Gills: Gray filoplume
Top of abdomen: Dark turkey tail
Rib: Gold wire

Front section:
Thorax: Tan-amber dubbing
Collar: Dark grouse body feather
Wingcase: Dark turkey tail
Head and eyes: Melted monofilament and
               tan-amber dubbing

This is Walt Grau's version of the Michigan mayfly nymph, *Hexagenia limbata*, that is so important to steelheading in the waters of that state. Nymphs using grouse or pheasant filo-plume feathers are the most realistic and effective. Grau feels that for Michigan steelhead Hexagenia nymphs are second in importance only to egg patterns.

Tied by Walt Grau

FLEA

Tied by Jim Rusher

Tail and wing: White poly yarn	Body: Fluorescent green chenille

Jim Rusher of Whitaker's Sport Shop in Pulaski, New York, sent us this pattern and confidently stated that for steelhead on the Salmon River it was one of the "... most effective patterns all around." Tied small, down to size 12 and 14, the best colors seem to be fluorescent green, black and light-blue chenilles, all with white poly yarn. The chenille body of a variation called the "Spawning Flea" is palmered with natural or dyed grizzly hackle and fished early in the run from mid October through November.

FLUORESCENT STONEFLY NYMPH

Tied by Greg Liu

Tail: Pearl crystal flash	Wingcase: Green braided Mylar
Abdomen: Fluorescent rose dubbing	Legs: Pearl crystal flash, three strands on each side of the thorax
Rib: A single strand of pearl crystal flash	
Thorax: Fluorescent rose dubbing	Head: Orange

"A favorite fly that I fish all the time" declares Greg Liu, a steelhead guide, who devised this nymph for the Salmon River in Pulaski, New York. Tied in a variety of colors and sizes depending on water conditions, it is both a colorful attractor and an impressionistic imitation of a natural stonefly.

FLUORESCENT WIGGLER

Tied by Dawn Gillis

Body: Fluorescent green chenille	Head: Glo-Bug yarn trimmed short, extending over the eye of the hook
Hackle: Yellow, palmered	
Wingcase: Flame Glo-Bug yarn	

This pattern was tied by Dawn Gillis of Gillis' Fly Fishing Shoppe in South Bend, Indiana. She and her husband Jim "found this fly in a streambed in 1981." Tied in the style of Spring's Wiggler, it has become one of the most popular and effective patterns sold in this shop for steelhead in Indiana and Michigan.

FREESTONE CADDIS

Tied by Dave Wixon

Body: Fluorescent pink chenille	Head: Black chenille
Collar: Black hackle, sparse	

A simple but effective caddis-larva imitation, Wayne Orzel, of Prichard's Western Angler designed this pattern for Washington's Kalama River in the mid 1970s. Many western rivers support healthy caddis populations, and bright, impressionistic caddis larva imitations produce excellent catches.

FREESTONE NYMPH

Tail:	Pearl crystal flash and black hackle barbs	Throat:	Pearl crystal flash
Abdomen:	Black seal fur or substitute	Collar:	Black hackle, in front of the throat
Rib:	Pearl crystal flash	Wingcase:	Pearl crystal flash, pulled over the thorax and the collar
Thorax:	Black seal or substitute		

Paul Noble of London, Ontario, originated this nymph in 1989 for the Saugeen and Ganaraska Rivers, freestone Canadian tributaries of Lake Huron and Lake Ontario respectively, and it fishes best in the spring or fall, or in water that is slightly cloudy.

Tied by Ian James

GIANT BLACK CRAWLER

Tail:	Black schlappen hackle barbs	Legs:	Several turns of long black schlappen, trimmed at the bottom
Abdomen:	Black rabbit fur dubbing	Antennae:	Several black schlappen fibers
Rib:	Black Swannundaze over the abdomen	Note:	The Giant Natural Crawler substitutes hare's ear dubbing for black rabbit
Thorax:	Australian opposum		
Wingcase:	Sections of dark turkey tail		

A creation of Dave Hall of Glide, Oregon, the crawler was first tied in 1983, during a summer when the fish on the North Umpqua were not taking traditional patterns well. It seemed logical to fish more natural looking flies to represent local nymphs. Throughout that year Hall's natural-looking nymph patterns produced fish and they continue to do so.

Tied by Dave Hall

H.B. STONE

Hook:	Caddis nymph hook	Legs:	Brown hackle palmered over the thorax
Tail:	Light brown goose biots	Wingcase:	Dark turkey tail
Abdomen:	Brown chenille	Note:	Usually weighted with lead wire
Thorax:	Brown chenille		

This is a simple dark stonefly nymph that was given to us by Dave Wixon who ties nymphs for Prichard's Western Angler in Washington state. In recent years the use of nymphs on west coast steelhead rivers has increased, with dark stonefly nymphs leading the way.

Tied by Dave Wixon

HALL'S FLASHBACK NYMPH

Tail:	Black hackle barbs with 2 to 4 strands of pearl Flashabou		men
		Wingcase:	Dark turkey tail
Body (abdomen and thorax):	Black rabbit fur dubbing	Hackle:	Black hackle barbs and a few strands of pearl Flashabou
Rib:	Pearl Flashabou over the abdo-	Head:	Black rabbit dubbing

Dave Hall of Umpqua Feather Merchants originated the "Flashback" in 1984. He considers this to be his basic all-purpose black steelhead nymph, and it is very effective on rivers that fish well with nymphs, like the North Umpqua and Kalama. Another fly called the Flashback Nymph was designed for trout fishing by Tim Tollett of Dillon, Montana, and uses flat silver Mylar as a wingcase material.

Tied by Dave Hall

Tied by Jay Passmore

JAY'S GREEN RAFFIA STONE

Tail:	Grizzly hackle barbs	Hackle:	Three turns of grizzly palmered over the thorax
Abdomen:	Fluorescent yellow dubbing		
Rib:	Copper wire	Wingcase:	Kelly green raffia (continued from the back)
Back:	Kelly green raffia (bound down by the copper wire)		
Thorax:	Fluorescent yellow dubbing	Head:	Fluorescent green

Developed in 1988 by professional fly tier Jay Passmore of J & B Tie-Master Tackle in Dungannon, Ontario, for summer- and fall-run steelhead, the Raffia Stone is popular in Canada on the Nottawasaga, Beaver, Big Head, Saugeen and Nine Mile Rivers, and probably just as effective on the U.S. side.

Tied by Jay Passmore

JAY'S ORIGAMI STONE

Tail:	Peccary fibers		Origami paper cut to shape
Underbody:	Appropriate Nymphorm wrapped with black wool	Legs:	Three brown hen hackle sections, tied under each wingcase
Abdomen:	Brown Tyvek Origami paper	Eyes:	Melted monofilament
Thorax:	Beige chenille	Head:	Brown, built up
Wingcase:	Three sections of brown Tyvek	Antennae:	Peccary

This fly is one of a series of steelhead stonefly nymphs tied in black, gold and brown and introduced by Jay Passmore of Dungannon, Ontario. They are very effective on the steelhead tributaries of Lake Ontario and Lake Huron. Tyvek Origami paper is very durable and gives the nymph a realistic appearance.

Tied by Jeff Wells

JEFF'S HEX

Tail:	Gray fluff from the base of a ring-neck pheasant body feather	Hackle:	A soft cream-colored ringneck pheasant body hackle, tied in by the tip and palmered forward over the thorax
Abdomen:	Cream dubbing or yarn		
Gills:	Gray barbs of a feather from the base of a cock ringneck pheasant tail		
		Wingcase:	Gray barbs from a ringneck cock pheasant tail
Rib:	Copper wire	Eyes:	Melted black monofilament
Thorax:	Cream dubbing or yarn	Head:	Cream fur dubbed around the eyes

This Hexagenia nymph was developed by Jeff Wells, who operates Jeff's Lake View Fly Shop, Lake Odessa, Michigan. The dressing was influenced by the Schmidt's Hex, with additional input from tier Jeff "Bear" Andrews.

Tied by Backcast Fly Shop

LATEX WIGGLER

Hook:	Caddis nymph or English bait	Hackle:	Brown, palmered along the edge of the latex strips
Tail:	Red squirrel tail or ringneck pheasant tail barbs		
		Back:	Ringneck pheasant tail barbs, red squirrel tail, or just mark the latex body with a brown marking pen
Body:	A narrow strip of natural latex sheeting		

This intersting variation of a Michigan wiggler was sent to us by the Backcast Fly Shop in Benzonia, Michigan. It is a very popular pattern in that area and is most effective in clear water. This fly was probably originated by Glen Dennison, but George Richey, Jim Conkright and others have contributed to its evolution.

MOSSBACK NYMPH

Tail (1): Short tuft of red yarn over which
are several strands of gold crystal
flash
Tail (2): Two strands of dark gray rubber
hackle
Body: Variegated green and black che-

nille, one turn under the tail (2),
over an optional base of lead wire
Rib: A single strand of gold crystal flash
Antennea: Two strands of dark gray rubber
hackle

A companion pattern to the popular Brindle Bug, the Mossback Nymph was originated for
the Klamath River by Austin McWithey of Happy Camp, California. The feeling among
many local anglers is that if the Brindle Bug doesn't work, the Mossback probably will.

Tied by Austin McWithey

OSCAR'S HEX

Tail: Soft brown ringneck pheasant tail
barbs
Underbody: Dental floss built into a tapered
body and flattened with pliers
Abdomen: Cream sparkle yarn
Rib: Oval gold tinsel
Abdomen top: Pheasant tail or mottled tur-
key, lacquered
Gills: A gray stem of down from a par-
tridge or pheasant, trimmed and

folded over the top of the abdomen before pulling the turkey or
pheasant tail over
Thorax: Orange sparkle yarn
Hackle: Brown hackle palmered over thorax and trimmed across bottom
Wingcase: Pheasant tail or mottled turkey,
lacquered
Head and eyes: Orange tying thread around
melted 15lb. monofilament eyes

A Hexagenia nymph by Chilean-born fly tyer Oscar Feliu.

Tied by Oscar Feliu

OSCAR'S RHYCOPHELIA

Hook: Caddis nymph hook
Body: Chartreuse Larva Lace over an underbody of dubbed gray rabbit fur;
the Larva Lace is applied in a man-
ner that allows some of the rabbit

guard hairs to stick out between
wraps
Legs: Dark deer hair
Thorax: Black rabbit dubbing

Oscar Feliu designed this realistic nymph and introduced it to the steelhead rivers of
Michigan in 1984. Feliu observed that during the commotion of digging nests and spawning
a sufficient number of caddis nymphs were dislodged to create a "manufactured hatch" that
attracted the attention of many steelhead. This is a durable, realistic and effective dressing.

Tied by Oscar Feliu

OSCAR'S RIBBON FOX

Tail: Soft, brown webby hackle barbs
and three ringneck pheasant tail
barbs
Underbody: Waxed dental floss, built up,
tapered and flattened with pliers
Abdomen: Gray red fox body fur

Rib: Oval gold tinsel
Thorax: Amber rabbit fur
Hackle: Two tufts of brown speckled par-
tridge on either the side of the head
Wingcase: Brown poly gift-wrap ribbon
Head: Light orange

Inspired by the success of the Hare's Ear nymph design, Oscar Feliu created this steelhead
nymph for Michigan waters. It features a wingpad formed from gift-wrapping ribbon made
of polypropylene, which helps maintain the fly in an upright position in the current.

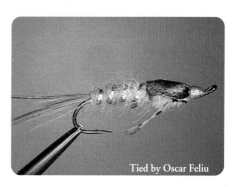
Tied by Oscar Feliu

Tied by Oscar Feliu

OSCAR'S TERROR

Tail: Brown hackle over which are three
            long, divided ringneck tail barbs
Underbody: Waxed dental floss, built-up
            into a cigar shape and flattened
Abdomen: Yellow floss with brown tail hackle
            butts pulled over the top; ribbed
            with a center feather from a pea-
            cock eye, lacquered, followed by
            center joint of peacock herl
Thorax: Orange-yellow sparkle yarn
Hackle: Brown hackle palmered over tho-
            rax and trimmed on the bottom
Wingcase: Mottled turkey tail, lacquered

In 1971, Oscar Feliu designed this as a trout-fly imitation of the basic Stenonema nymph for the freestone rivers of Michigan. In the spring of 1986 he began fishing it for steelhead on the tributaries of Lake Ontario where it is very productive.

Tied by Peter Micol

P.M. BRASSIE

Hook: Usually tied on a small dry fly
         hook
Tail: Purple bucktail, long and fine
Body: Copper wire
Thorax: Purple dubbing
Collar: One or two turns of purple hackle

This is a variation of the famous trout Brassie. It is a caddis pupa imitation designed by steelheader Peter Micol for the clear water of Michigan's Pere Marquette River. Micol enjoys good success with small flies that are sparsely dressed, using dry-fly hooks rarely larger than a size 10. It is interesting to note that during the 1930s and 40s a series of steelhead patterns with bodies of copper or brass wire, was developed by Peter Schwab of Yreka, California.

Tied by Jeff "Bear" Andrews

P.M.S. BLACK

Tail: Soft black hackle barbs
Abdomen: Black dubbing over which is
            dark turkey tail coated with vinyl
            cement and ribbed with fine gold
            wire
Thorax: Peacock herl
Wingcase: Dark turkey tail coated with vi-
            nyl cement
Throat: Natural soft black hackle applied
            as a collar and folded back

The P.M.S. (Pere Marquette Stonefly) is a tremendously effective and popular nymph pattern for the clear tributaries of Lake Michigan. It was designed by professional fly tier Jeff "Bear" Andrews of Grand Ledge, Michigan and is tied in a variety of neutral shades including olive and brown.

Tied by Kaufmann's Streamborn

R.K. STONE NYMPH, BLACK

Hook: 6x long streamer hook that is
            weighted heavily with lead wire
            and flattened with pliers
Tail: Short black goose biots
Abdomen: A mixture of 40% black Haretron
            and 10% each of purple, claret,
            brown, blue, orange and black
            angora
Rib: Clear-smoke Swannundaze over
            the abdomen
Wingcase: Dark turkey tail, lacquered, cut
            to a "V" shape and applied in three
            segments as shown, with dubbing
            between
Thorax: Same mixture as abdomen, well
            picked out for legs
Antennae: Black goose biots

"R.K." stands for Randall Kaufmann, author of *American Nymph Fly Tying Manual* and *The Fly Tyers Nymph Manual*. Although he originated this nymph for trout, it has become quite popular as a steelhead fly and is tied in several colors.

RICHARDS' HEX

Rear section:
Tail: Ringneck pheasant tail barbs
Abdomen: Light tan spun fur
Gills: Gray aftershafts (the small, fluffy body feathers found near the base of a larger feather; often called filoplumes)
Rib: Nylon thread dyed amber

Front section:
Thorax: Light tan spun fur
Gills: Gray aftershafts (filoplume)
Legs: Brown partridge
Wingcase: Mottled turkey wing quill segment

This articulated wiggle nymph was tied by Carl Richards of Rockford, Michigan. This fly-construction technique was introduced in 1971 in *Selective Trout,* the first of the books that Richards co-authored with Doug Swisher.

Tied by Carl Richards

RUSTY CADDIS PUPA

Body: Loosely dubbed rusty seal fur or substitute, over an underbody of red-orange chenille
Collar: Brown partridge body hackle

Wing: A few ringneck pheasant tail barbs
Head: Dubbed black marabou, black ostrich or peacock herl

Mark Noble of Vancouver, Washington, tied this fly in 1980 for the Trinity and Klamath Rivers of northern California where it proved highly effective. Over the years it has been an excellent late-season pattern on most rivers that have large caddis populations. Fish it deep during the winter, and at or near the surface during the late summer and fall.

Tied by Mark Noble

SALMON RIVER CADDIS

Abdomen: Olive crystal chenille
Thorax: Black pearl Estaz chenille
Head: Fluorescent green

Note: Also often tied with an abdomen of burnt orange or light green crystal chenille

An effective steelhead caddis originally dressed by Fran Verdoliva of Mexico, New York, for the Salmon River, it is best when fished "on a dead drift during late fall and winter."

Tied by Fran Verdoliva

SALMON RIVER SPRING WIGGLER

Body: Orange crystal chenille
Tail and shellback: Gray squirrel tail, dyed

orange, secured at the tail and head

This is a local adaptation of the "Spring's Wiggler," a classic Michigan steelhead pattern designed in the 1960s. Popular combinations for the Salmon River and other tributaries of eastern Lake Ontario include peacock herl with natural red squirrel, pearlescent chenille and a variety of natural and dyed squirrel tails.

Tied by Fran Verdoliva

Tied by Fran Verdoliva

SALMON RIVER STONEFLY

Tail:	Black goose biots, tied long	Head:	Orange
Abdomen:	Black crystal chenille or trimmed Estaz chenille	Note:	Tied in brown and yellow, or in more impressionistic colors such as pink, fluorescent green or orange
Wingcase:	Purple Diamond Braid		
Thorax:	Black pearl Estaz chenille		

Stoneflies represent a significant portion of the arsenal of Lake Ontario steelhead guide and fly originator, Fran Verdoliva. In the spring and fall he prefers large stonefly imitations, but during the winter when the water is clear and often low he prefers small, dark flies.

Tied by Farrow Allen

SCHAADT'S FEELER NYMPH

Tail:	Teal flank barbs	Wing:	Grizzly hackle tips dyed orange
Body:	Brown wool	Collar:	Brown hackle
Rib:	Brown thread	Head:	Tan

This is one of many simple nymphs dating back to the 1950s that were originated on the Russian River by northern California angler Bill Schaadt. These patterns are specifically designed for conditions when steelhead are schooled up and skittish, and they work best when tied down to sizes 12 and 14, fished on a long, super-fine leader.

Tied by Ray Schmidt

SCHMIDT'S HEX NYMPH

Hook:	Straight eye streamer hook	Legs:	A few turns of a mottled brown hen back feather
Tail and back:	Barbs from the tail of a ringneck pheasant	Wingcase:	Ringneck pheasant tail barbs
Abdomen and thorax:	Tan-gray dubbing	Eyes:	Melted black monofilament
Rib:	Copper wire over the abdomen and binding down the pheasant tail barbs over the abdomen	Note:	Often weighted with wraps of lead wire

Originated in 1978 by Ray Schmidt, a well-known steelhead guide from Wellston, Michigan. Like many other realistic Hexagenia nymphs, this one is a reliable producer from November through April on the Manistee, Little Manistee and Pere Marquette Rivers in Michigan.

SCHMIDT'S RHYCOPHELIA CADDIS LARVA

Hook:	Short shank or caddis style		yarn
Body:	Bright green Antron dubbing or	Thorax:	Peacock herl

Imitations of the bright-green Rhycophelia caddisfly larva are of major significance on most Michigan steelhead rivers. This is a simple representative dressing that steelhead guide Ray Schmidt developed for the Manistee River in 1981. It is best fished dead drift along the bottom in September and October, but it can also be effective during the spring if the water is not too high and discolored.

SOUTH PLATTE BRASSIE

Tail:	Fine natural bucktail tips	Collar:	Yellow hackle
Body:	Brass wire	Head:	Fluorescent red

This fly was sent to us by Leon Hanson, a rod builder and serious steelhead fisherman from Plymouth, Michigan, who uses it successfully in low water over steelhead that have been "fished hard." He does not use any cement in the construction of his flies. "I can smell it and I know they can." The Brassie is usually tied small, in sizes 10 to 14.

Tied by Leon Hanson

SPARKLE GIRDLE BUG

Tail:	White rubber hackle	Antennae:	White rubber hackle
Abdomen:	Black crystal chenille	Head:	Fluorescent orange
Thorax:	Orange Estaz chenille		

A flashy New York steelhead variation of a western trout fly which was initially tied as a heavily-weighted imitation of the western giant-black stonefly. The original Girdle Bug is somewhat like the Ugly Bug (which see). Steelhead guide Greg Liu, the designer of this version, describes his pattern as "a good flashy fly to roll along the bottom."

Tied by Greg Liu

SPRING'S WIGGLER

Tail:	Gray squirrel tail dyed orange	Shellback:	Gray squirrel tail dyed orange, folded forward over the top and trimmed as shown
Body:	Orange chenille (fluorescent lime green is an effective variation)		
Hackle:	Fluorescent orange	Head:	Fluorescent orange

The Spring's Wiggler (often called Spring Wiggler) was originated by Frank and Ron Spring of Muskegon, Michigan, during the 1960s. It roughly imitates the prolific giant Michigan mayfly *(Hexagenia limbata)*, abundant on many midwest steelhead rivers, and was originally tied with a tail and shellback of red squirrel tail, a yellow chenille body and a furnace hackle. Along with various egg patterns, the Wiggler is one of the most effective flies on these rivers for the winter-run fish that comprise the bulk of the fishery.

Tied by Jeff "Bear" Andrews

STEELHEAD STONEFLY NYMPH

Tail:	Black goose biots	Thorax:	Black (or red as a variation) dubbing or poly yarn over an optional base of lead wire
Abdomen:	Black poly yarn bound with a copper wire rib and attached to the hook shank		
Legs:	Black braided fishing line, dubbed at the base (femur) with black fur	Wingcase:	Black poly yarn, separated into three segments
		Antennae:	Black braided fishing line

This large nymph was developed in 1987 by Dan Cottrell of Edmonton, Alberta. It has proved to be effective on the Skeena, Copper, Thompson and Bulkley Rivers. These British Columbia freestone rivers support many stoneflies which provide food for young steelhead before they go to sea. When they return to spawn they are often susceptible to stonefly imitations.

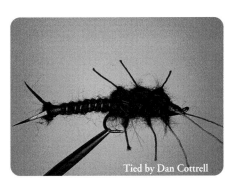
Tied by Dan Cottrell

SYDENHAM PEACOCK

Tied by Jay Passmore

Tail: Black hackle barbs
Abdomen: Peacock herl
Rib: Copper wire over the abdomen
Thorax: Peacock herl over a base of lead

wire
Wingcase: Turkey wing quill dyed black
Legs: Turkey wing quill barbs, dyed black
           and split to each side

This simple nymph pattern was designed in 1983 by Jim Weir of Guelph, Ontario, for fishing on the Sydenham River, a tributary flowing into Lake Huron's Georgian Bay. It is a well-known steelhead pattern in Ontario and is effective for those anglers who are willing to fish from December into spring.

TEENY NYMPH

Tied by Teeny Nymph Co.

Body: Dyed or natural ringneck pheas-
         ant tail barbs wrapped around the
         hook
Throat: Remainder of pheasant barbs
         pulled down and secured below

the hook
Note: On hooks of size 4 and larger, the
         body is usually formed in two equal
         sections with two separate beards

This is the first of several popular and effective fly patterns designed by Jim Teeny of the Teeny Nymph Company in Gresham, Oregon. It was originated in 1962 for trout fishing in stillwater along the shoreline of Oregon's East Lake, and has grown steadily in popularity as a steelhead fly. Teeny ties it in a variety of colors ranging from subued black and insect green to flame orange.

UGLY BUG

Tied by Brad Jackson

Tail: Two gray-black rubber hackles
Underbody: Lead wire double-wrapped in
            the thorax to enhance the nymph
            shape

Body: Black chenille
Hackle: Three pair of gray-black rubber
           hackles
Antennae: Gray-black rubber hackle

This fly was designed in 1976 by Brad Jackson of Redding, California, and is commonly referred to as Brad Jackson's Ugly Bug. It is a killer on rivers like the Trinity, Kalama, McKenzie and North Umpqua where steelhead hold in the fast deep runs and respond well to nymphs and leech patterns fished deep on a dead drift. The Girdle Bug is a nearly identical fly that features white rubber legs instead of gray, and it's often ribbed with silver tinsel.

ULTRA STONE, BLACK

Tied by Dave Wixon

Hook: Caddis larva
Tail: Black goose biots
Underbody: Furry Foam or wool
Abdomen: A tapered strip of black "Ultra
           Leather" a rubberized matte vinyl
           craft material, applied with over-
           lapping wraps

Thorax: Black fur or wool
Hackle: Several turns of natural soft black
          hackle
Wingcase: A wedge shaped piece of black
           Ultra Leather, optionally etched
           in the design of a wingcase with a
           hot needle

Dave Wixon, a part-time commercial fly tier from Seattle who specializes in steelhead nymphs, originated this pattern. On those weekends when he's not fishing, Wixon can often be found tying flies in the back of Prichard's Western Anglers shop on the Kalama River where his stonefly nymphs are very popular.

WALT'S FLASHBACK STONE

Tail: Black rubber hackle
Abdomen: Black fur dubbing
Rib: Black Swannundaze
Thorax: Black fur dubbing, picked out to

imitate legs
Wingcase: Copper Flashabou
Head: Black fur dubbing
Antennae: Black rubber hackle

This is Walt Grau's version of the popular "Flashback Nymph," all of which use some form of flashy synthetic material as the wingcase. It is interesting to note that in the 1940s John Atherton was experimenting with iridescent English kingfisher feathers to "suggest the sparkle of color or light on the wingcases" of his nymphs.

Tied by Walt Grau

WHITE WIGGLE STONE

Rear section: Silver straight-eye hook, trimmed at the bend, and connected to the front hook with stiff monofilament
Tail: White rubber hackle
Body: Cream dubbing

Rib: Transparent amber Swannundaze
Thorax: Cream dubbing, picked out to imitate legs
Wingcase: Tan nylon raffia
Head: Cream dubbing
Antennae: White rubber hackle

This is an "albino version of a molting yellow stonefly" tied by steelhead guide Walt Grau of Baldwin, Michigan. Grau credits fellow angler Kelley Gallup of Traverse City, Michigan, for proving to him the value of such an imitation during the winter of 1986-87.

Tied by Walt Grau

WINAN'S WIGGLER

Tail: Orange calftail
Body: Yellow-orange chenille
Hackle: Red saddle palmered over the body

Shellback: Orange calftail
Head: Red

Originated in 1971 by George Richey, a fly tier and outdoor writer from Honor, Michigan, this fly was named for Larry Winan, a frequent fishing partner of Richey's. It is a bright variation of the Spring's Wiggler that works well early in the season or when steelhead are on the spawning beds.

Tied by George Richey

WOOLY WORM

Tail: Red yarn or a short tuft of red marabou
Body: Black chenille
Hackle: Soft grizzly, palmered

Head: Red
Note: Wooly worms are tied in a wide range of colors

The Wooly Worm is an enormously popular trout fly which is also productive for steelhead on both western and midwestern rivers. Leo Lavigne, an angler from Vermont described sight fishing to steelhead in the Pere Marquette River in the early 1970s, saying that it appeared the fish recognized the danger of his presence yet they were so attracted to his size 10 Wooly Worm they rushed it with abandon, hoping to capture it before being discovered.

Tied by Kent Bulfinch

Tied by Clair Groulx

ADMIRAL

Tail:	Red hackle barbs or hair	Throat:	Red hackle, pulled back
Body:	Red wool	Wing:	White calftail or bucktail
Rib:	Oval gold tinsel		

The Admiral was originally designed as a rainbow-trout fly, but was found to be very effective for migrating steelhead. This dressing is a hairwing variation of the fly originated by Rear Admiral E.B. Rogers. He tied the Admiral with scarlet silk floss and white goose-quill wings.

Tied by Mark Noble

AFTER DINNER MINT

Tail:	Black hackle barbs (optional)		purple over which is black marabou
Body:	Green Mylar Poly-Flash or Diamond Braid	Head:	Black deer body hair spun and clipped to form a traditional Muddler Minnow type head and collar
Wing:	A few strands of pearl crystal flash over which is gray squirrel tail dyed		

The After Dinner Mint is the popular dark companion of the hairwing "Natural Mint" that was originated in the mid 1980s by Mark Noble of the Greased Line Fly Shoppe in Vancouver, Washington. The "Mint" series, of which there are many variations, is used throughout the season from Oregon's North Umpqua to the Dean River in British Columbia.

Tied by Bob Aid

AID'S RED AND ORANGE MARABOU

Body:	Flat silver Mylar tinsel		tied in by the tip and wound as a collar in front of the dubbing
Shoulder:	Ball of orange seal fur dubbing or substitute	Collar:	Teal or guinea fowl
Hackle:	Orange followed by red marabou,		

This is the first in a series of marabou patterns from Bob Aid who manages Kaufmann's Streamborn Flies in downtown Seattle. In the early 1980s Aid developed this and several other flies (see Skagit Special) from patterns tied by John Farrar. Farrar forms a loop and applies the marabou like dubbing. Aid, who finds the Farrar technique time-consuming, wraps his marabou-like hackle to achieve a non-fouling marabou pattern (see Farrar Marabou).

Tied by Russ Miller

AL'S SPECIAL

Tag:	Oval silver tinsel	Throat:	Several turns of red hackle, pulled back
Tail:	Red hackle barbs		
Body:	Yellow chenille	Wing:	White bucktail
Rib:	Oval silver tinsel		

This fly was originated by the late Al Knudsen, a professional fly tier from Everett, Washington. Knudsen is best known for his spiders which were tied with long, soft collars of mallard flank (see Knudsen's Spider) and his pioneering use of extremely large streamers for winter steelhead fishing in the 1930s.

ALASKA MARY ANN

Tail:	Red hackle barbs	Wing:	White polar bear, calftail or bucktail
Body:	White chenille		
Rib:	Fine oval silver tinsel or wire	Cheeks:	Jungle cock

The Alaska Mary Ann is a classic fly that was first tied in the 1920s by Frank Dufresne. His inspiration reportedly came from a red-and-white carved-ivory ice-fishing lure used by Alaskan Eskimos in the Kubok River region. A renowned sportsman, Dufresne served as fish-and-game commissioner of Alaska and later worked for the U.S. Fish and Wildlife Service.

Tied by Wayne Orzel

ALEXANDRA

Tail:	Red goose wing quill segment	Wing:	Peacock sword
Body:	Flat silver tinsel	Sides:	Red goose wing quill segment, the length of the wing
Rib:	Oval silver tinsel		
Collar:	Soft black hackle, tied full		

The Alexandra is a 19th-century British trout pattern that Canadian anglers found to be very effective for steelhead entering rivers on the Canadian side of Lake Ontario. It is most often tied as a streamer and fished in riffles and at the mouths of rivers where steelhead often congregate.

Tied by Ian James

ASSASSIN

Body:	Dark olive dubbing, yarn or floss		palmered forward
Rib:	Oval gold tinsel	Wing:	About eight strands of lime green or pearl crystal flash, tied short
Hackle:	Brown saddle tied in by the tip and		

This simple Wooly Worm pattern was introduced by Dale Lackey on California's Klamath and Trinity Rivers in 1985. Lackey, a guide on the Lower Klamath, says that the Assassin is frequently tied low-water style and is most effective for summer steelhead.

Tied by Dale Lackey

BEAR'S FLASH BACK

Tail:	Black hen hackle barbs		tal hair shellback
Body:	Fuzzy black yarn	Collar:	Soft black hackle
Shellback:	Blue-green peacock crystal flash	Eyes:	Silver bead-chain eyes
Rib:	Blue wire, binding down the crys-		

Jeff "Bear" Andrews of Grand Ledge, Michigan, developed this extremely popular pattern. Although there are a number "Flashback" patterns that feature wingcases of Flashabou or crystal flash, this one has been remarkably reliable.

Tied by Jeff "Bear" Andrews

BEDSPRINGS SPEY

Tied by John Shewey

Tag:	Flat gold tinsel and fluorescent orange floss	Rib:	Flat gold followed by oval gold
Tail:	Golden pheasant crest dyed orange	Hackle:	Black Spey, palmered over the brown seal
Body:	Rear ½: Orange seal fur dubbing	Collar:	Teal dyed brown
	Front ½: Brown seal fur dubbing	Wing:	Bronze mallard sections
		Head:	Orange

A "wicked" looking dark fly, this Spey pattern was developed by John Shewey of Aumsville, Oregon for fishing the Deschutes River, where combinations of black, orange and brown are generally productive. Designed for slower resting lies and named after a pool on the Deschutes where an old set of bedsprings adorn the river bank.

BLACK ARTICULATED LEECH

Tied by Marty Sherman

Back hook:		Note:	Each body is tied over a heavy black loop of braided dacron fishing line which is used to connect the two parts
Body:	Black yarn, followed by a middle joint of black marabou, wrapped 360°, followed by black yarn followed by black marabou wrapped 360°, over which is black crystal hair	Front hook (hook shank only, the point and bend are removed):	
		Body:	Same as back hook

This pattern was recommended to us by Marty Sherman, editor of *Flyfishing* magazine and a very experienced steelheader. The fly is deadly on most rivers in British Columbia, and it's usually tied quite large, up to 4 inches long.

BLACK DIAMOND

Tied by Harry Lemire

Tag:	Flat silver tinsel		as a collar)
Body:	Black dubbing	Wing:	About four peacock sword barbs over which is a sparse mixture of gray squirrel tail and guinea fowl barbs
Rib:	Flat silver tinsel		
Throat:	Guinea fowl hackle as a beard (if jungle cock is omitted wind one complete turn of guinea fowl hackle	Cheeks:	Jungle cock (optional)

The Black Diamond was originated by Harry Lemire around 1963 and named for his home town in Washington. It is a tidy, dark fly that is especially effective in shallow tailouts during the summer and fall when fished using the greased-line technique.

BLACK GORDON

Tied by Joe Howell

Butt:	Oval gold tinsel	Rib:	Oval gold tinsel
Body:	Rear ⅓: Red yarn	Collar:	Black hackle
	Front ⅔: Black yarn	Wing:	Black hair

The Black Gordon was originated by Clarence Gordon, a well-known guide and manager of the North Umpqua's Steamboat Lodge during the 1940s. It was first tied in the mid 1930s and is still fished on the North Umpqua, throughout southern Oregon, and into northern California.

BLACK HERON

Body:	Rear ⅔: Flat silver tinsel
	Front ⅓: Black seal fur or substitute
Rib:	Oval silver tinsel over both portions of the body
Hackle:	Gray heron substitute, dyed black, with one side stripped away, palmered forward over the dubbing only
Throat:	Guinea fowl wound as a collar and pulled down and back
Wing:	Matching black goose shoulder quills (originally heron), set low and tent style over the body

This is a Syd Glasso pattern that is known as a Silver Heron when it's tied with a gray wing. Our fly was tied by Bob Veverka of Underhill, Vermont, who has spent many years studying Glasso's flies. Veverka suggests that schlappen, coot, or dyed or natural rump feathers from various species of pheasants may be used as legal substitutes for heron.

Tied by Bob Veverka

BLACK KRAHE SPEY

Body:	Black squirrel fur or substitute
Rib:	Fine oval silver tinsel
Hackle:	Black Spey hackle
Throat:	Guinea fowl barbs
Wing:	Segments of silver pheasant wing quill, set low

This is a favorite steelhead fly originated by Tim Krahe, an active fisherman and fly tier from Manistee, Michigan. It is an easy-to-tie dark Spey pattern that accounts for many fish throughout the season.

Tied by Tim Krahe

BLACK MAGIC

Tag:	Oval silver tinsel
Body:	Black Antron yarn or dubbing, dressed full and buggy
Rib:	Oval silver tinsel, reverse wrapped
Wing:	Black bear hair

This fly was submitted by Tony Petrella of Lansing, Michigan. It is simple but effective and easy to tie. On the Pere Marquette, where it is principally fished, it works best early in the morning and in the evening. A nearly-identical pattern introduced in 1975 by Eugene Sunday of Flushing, Michigan, on the Upper Peninsula, is equally effective tied all brown and works well on heavily-fished water during the spring.

Tied by Tony Petrella

BLACK PRINCE

Tail:	Red hackle barbs
Body:	Rear ⅓: Yellow wool
	Front ⅔: Black chenille or wool
Rib:	Oval silver tinsel
Wing:	Black bucktail
Collar:	Black hackle

The Black Prince is an old pattern from the North Umpqua that retains a surprising degree of popularity considering that it dates back to the late 1800s. It is similar in style to Clarence Gordon's Black Gordon although its originator is unknown.

Tied by Bill Logan

Tied by Al Doll

BLUE MUTHER

Body:	Pearl braided Mylar	Collar:	Purple hackle
Wing:	Blue calftail	Head:	Red

The Blue Muther was originated in the late 1970s by Al Doll, a long-time commercial fly tier and river guide from Lansing, Michigan. This fly is best known for its successes on the Little Manistee River and is often fished together with a single-egg pattern as a dropper.

Tied by Farrow Allen

BLUE SKY

Tag:	Oval silver tinsel	Wing:	Dyed blue hackle tips curving out-ward
Tail:	Blue hackle barbs		
Body:	Blue yarn or floss	Collar:	Long soft blue hackle, tied behind and in front of the wing
Rib:	Oval silver tinsel		

Stan Young of Bellevue, Washington, who retired from the National Park Service in 1982 and devotes his free time to pursuing steelhead from southern Oregon to British Columbia, originated this fly. It is his most dependable pattern and he fishes in sizes 1/0 to 10 ". . . on all rivers and during all seasons and under all water conditions."

Tied by Ian James

BLUE THUNDER

Body:	Flat silver tinsel	Wing:	White calftail over which is purple Flashabou
Rib:	Oval silver tinsel		

This, and a similar pattern with a red-Flashabou overwing called the Dexter, were introduced in 1984 by Ian James, a fly tier and steelhead guide from Guelph, Ontario. James noted that the spin fishermen were catching steelhead with a particular lure and he proceeded to tie a fly using the same color combinations. It works best in clear, low water, tied in small sizes.

Tied by Walt Grau

BLUEBERG

Body:	Blue Diamond Braid	Overwing: One mallard flank feather
Underwing:	White calftail or similar hair	Collar: Medium ginger hackle

Originated in 1986 by steelhead guide John Kluesing from Baldwin, Michigan, the Blueberg has turned out to be an excellent steelhead fly. It's invention was quite by accident. As guide Walt Grau describes it, Kluesing sat down one evening to "re-supply himself with Hornbergs." Finding himself out of practically everything required to dress a proper fly he began to substitute and the Blueberg resulted.

BOSS

Tail:	Black bucktail, long		ange hackle, long and tied slightly
Body:	Black chenille		back
Rib:	Oval silver tinsel	Eyes:	Silver bead chain
Collar:	Fluorescent or regular red or or-		

The now-famous Boss was popularized by Grant King of Guerenville, California, who owned a fly shop that he managed with his wife Betty. It is reported that he named this pattern for her - The Boss. The style of this fly was adapted from the original Comet (which see). The Boss series of flies have black tails, and often tend to be dressed more fully and are a bit heavier than the Comets. These features have led to some speculation that the Boss imitates the elver, or young eel.

Tied by André Puyans

BOSS, PURPLE

Tail:	Black hair, long	Collar:	Purple hackle, long and tied
Body:	Purple chenille		slightly back
Rib:	Oval silver tinsel	Eyes:	Silver bead chain

In 1963 André Puyans tied this purple version of the Boss based on the great success that bass fishermen had been having with that color. Almost thirty years later it has survived the test of time; in fact, purple is more popular than ever for steelhead flies.

Tied by André Puyans

BRAD'S BRAT

Tag:	Flat gold tinsel	Collar:	Brown hackle
Tail:	White and orange bucktail	Wing:	Bunch of white bucktail over
Body:	Rear ½: Orange wool		which is a smaller bunch of or-
	Front ½: Red wool		ange bucktail
Rib:	Flat gold tinsel		

This pattern was devised by Enos Bradner, the former outdoor editor of the *Seattle Times*, and introduced on Washington's Stillaguamish around 1937. It continues to be a popular fly for both winter- and summer-run fish.

Tied by Farrow Allen

BUNNY LEECH, PURPLE

Tail:	A few strands of purple crystal		cut) tied in at the tail and wrapped
	flash		forward tightly
Tail:	Purple rabbit fur strip, short	Wing:	Purple crystal flash
Body:	Purple rabbit fur strip (transverse	Head:	Fluorescent orange

This pattern was given to us by Joe Howell and is similar to Bob Borden's Bunny Bugger. The Bunny Leech may be tied in a variety of colors or color combinations, although black and purple are two of the best. Howell suggests that it should be weighted with lead wire.

Tied by Joe Howell

Tied by Kent Bulfinch

BURLAP

Tail:	Gray or light tan natural deer hair (coastal blacktail deer) tied fairly heavy
Body:	Burlap fiber tied full and rough-

ened to look shaggy
Collar: Slightly oversize soft grizzly hackle
Head: Gray

The popular Burlap was designed in 1945 by Arnold Arana of Dunsmuir, California, for the Klamath River where it is still a reliable producer. This neutral-color pattern is often weighted with lead wire. A popular variation from British Columbia is known as the Sack Fly and substitutes a tail of bright-orange hackle fibers.

Tied by Farrow Allen

CHAPPIE

Tail:	Grizzly hackle tips
Body:	Orange wool
Rib:	Orange silk thread or fine gold tinsel
Collar:	Grizzly hackle as long as the body
Wing:	Two grizzly hackles tied back to back, set high, extending beyond the bend of the hook
Head:	Orange

C.L. Franklin, who wrote an outdoor column for the *Los Angeles Times,* developed the Chappie around 1940 for summer-run steelhead. It is still a good fly on many rivers including the Grande Ronde and Wenatchee in Washington, the Clearwater in Idaho, and the Klamath in California. Elsewhere it is popular for sea-run cutthroat trout.

Tied by Mike McCoy

CLARET GUINEA

Tag:	Flat gold tinsel
Body:	Claret wool
Rib:	Oval gold tinsel
Hackle:	Purple, palmered forward along the tinsel rib, from the second turn
Collar:	Ringneck pheasant rump feather, dyed claret, in front of which is a turn of finely speckled guinea fowl
Head:	Claret

We were introduced to this pattern by Mike McCoy of Bothell, Washington, an avid steelheader, fly tier and importer of Chinese fly-tying silk. Although it was tied specifically for the Skykomish River, it has been effective on many other rivers from late spring through early fall.

Tied by Dick Stewart

COAL CAR

Tail:	Black hackle barbs
Body:	¼ fluorescent red-orange yarn ¼ fluorescent red yarn ½ black chenille
Rib:	Fine oval silver tinsel
Collar:	Soft black hackle
Wing:	A few strands of black crystal flash over which is black squirrel tail

Randall Kaufmann designed the Coal Car as a darker variation of his popular Freight Train and Krystal Flash Freight Train. The original flies were tied without the crystal flash which is now a standard part of this pattern. It is a consummate black fly - most effective on dark and overcast days or at dusk - that does not spook fish but carries enough color to engage their attention (see Coal Car Damp).

COMET

Tail:	Bright orange hair about 1½ times the length of the hook	Collar:	Bright orange hackle
		Eyes:	Silver bead chain (optional)
Body:	Oval silver tinsel		

In northern California, Lloyd Silvius tied this original Comet which launched both the Comet and the Boss series of flies. The first examples were tied with or without bead chain eyes, whereas later versions universally included the eyes. This orange version, and the Gold Comet, proved to be the most popular. Tied for winter use, the idea was that the fly would ride upside-down so it could be fished deep without snagging on the bottom.

Tied by Lloyd Silvius

COMET, BLACK FLASHABOU

Tail:	Black hen hackle barbs	Wingcase:	Pearl crystal flash
Body:	Black mohair	Collar:	Soft black hackle
Rib:	Single strand of pearl crystal flash	Eyes:	Silver bead chain

This Comet variation was introduced in about 1982 by Al Doll of Lansing, Michigan. Over the years it has proved to be an effective pattern for steelhead that are holding tight and hugging the bottom.

Tied by Frank Lendzion

COMET, GARY'S ESTAZ

Tail:	Orange bucktail	Collar:	Orange hackle, one side stripped of barbs
Butt:	Fluorescent red thread		
Body:	Rear ⅓: Flat silver tinsel	Eyes:	Small silver bead chain
	Front ⅔: Orange Estaz chenille	Head:	Fluorescent red

This pattern was originated by Gary Selig, a commercial steelhead and Atlantic-salmon fly tier from Mertztown, Pennsylvania. Selig spends most of his free time fishing the steelhead rivers along the eastern shore of Lake Ontario. This new pattern has proved very productive for fall and early winter fishing.

Tied by Gary Selig

COMET, P.M.

Hook:	Short shank silver	Collar:	Red and pink schlappen hackle, wound together
Tail:	White calftail		
Body:	Oval silver tinsel, including a few turns behind the tail	Eyes:	Large silver bead chain eyes secured in place with red thread

"P.M." is an abbreviation for Pere Marquette, the river where this fly was developed. It was designed in the traditional Comet style by Paul Goodman of Benchmark Outdoor Outfitters in Farmington, Michigan, and John Maxi, a highly-regarded Michigan steelheader who has spent much time on western steelhead rivers as well. The short hook and color of the P.M. Comet is well suited to the needs of Michigan steelheaders.

Tied by Paul Goodman

COON MUDDLER

Tied by Joe Howell

Body:	Gold Diamond Braid, Poly Flash, or oval gold tinsel		raccoon body hair
Wing:	Black and white barred woodduck over which is white-tipped	Head:	Spun deer or caribou body hair clipped to form a head and collar

The Coon Muddler was originated on the North Umpqua by Joe Howell in 1973 as an alternative to the standard Muddler Minnow that always proved deadly on this river. It is one of the few flies that uses raccoon hair. In the early 1970s, mottled turkey became scarce and Howell began looking for a Muddler-wing substitute that would appeal to steelhead. This fly works well fished deep or skated on the surface using a riffling hitch.

CRAZY CHARLIE

Tied by Farrow Allen

Hook:	Mustad 34007	Wing:	Fluorescent pink calftail over pearl Flashabou
Body:	Clear or pink Swannundaze over fluorescent red yarn	Eyes:	Silver bead chain

In the late 1980s steelheaders Michael Villanti and Gordy Carroll from Vermont were intrigued by a bin of bonefish flies at their local fly shop. They engaged the house tier, Charlie Lovelette, to tie up a bunch in smaller sizes, which they felt would be more suitable for Great Lakes steelhead. They were right; the flies proved to be deadly change-of-pace patterns and they have continued to fish them with great success. Meanwhile, on the west coast some anglers took the original Bob Nauheim design and adapted it to their steelheading needs. Idaho's Bob Wagoner even fashioned a series using Edge Brite for the bodies.

CRICK

Tied by George Richey

Tail:	Black calftail	Throat:	Black calftail
Body:	Rear ⅓: Fluorescent pink chenille	Wing:	White calftail over which is black calftail
	Front ⅔: Black chenille		

During the early 1970s George Richey of Honor, Michigan, spent several years developing this midwestern pattern. It was designed for, and fishes best in, high dirty water.

CUMMINGS SPECIAL

Tied by Bill Logan

Body:	Rear ⅓: Yellow-orange floss or wool	Collar:	Claret hackle
	Front ⅔: Claret wool or dubbing	Wing:	Brown bucktail or substitute
Rib:	Oval gold tinsel	Cheeks:	Jungle cock (optional)

The Cummings Special was a 1930s collaboration of Clarence Gordon, manager of a well-known steelhead fishing camp on the North Fork, and Ward Cummings, a popular guide on the Umpqua River in Oregon. Cummings is remembered for having tutored Ray Bergman in the mysteries of steelhead fishing.

DARK CADDIS

Body:	Burnt orange floss		palmered over the body
Hackle:	Coachman brown or dark brown	Wing:	Dark deer body hair

The Dark Caddis is often tied on a double hook and it's fished on a sink-tip line on the Rogue River for summer steelhead. On the Rogue, many guides consider this one of their top producing flies. There is also an older Mike Kennedy wet fly of the same name that is similar in color.

Tied by Gerald Jamos

DARK DAZE

Body:	Black fur dubbing	Throat:	Grass green hackle
Rib:	Flat green Mylar tinsel	Wing:	Pair of pheasant flank feathers dyed
Hackle:	Palmered black saddle hackle		black

This fly was designed by Mike Kinney of Oso, Washington, for fishing dark and overcast days on the Stillaguamish and Skagit Rivers. Kinney lives in a cabin on the banks of the Stillaguamish, fishes it daily and respects and understands it better than most. In a 1990 article in *Flyfishing*, Bob Arnold wrote of Kinney: "To many he is the Old Man of the River . . . he serves as their river keeper."

Tied by Mark Waslick

DAVE'S FAVORITE

Tail:	Dark yellow calftail	Wing:	Red calftail over which is dark
Body:	Fluorescent orange chenille		yellow calftail
Throat:	Dark yellow calftail	Head:	Red

Originated by George Richey of Honor, Michigan, in 1967 during the days when he was guiding for steelhead with his brother Dave. This fly was a favorite of both men, but especially for Dave, an outdoor writer and the author of several books, including *Steelheading for Everybody*.

Tied by George Richey

DAVE'S MISTAKE

Tag:	Flat silver tinsel	Wing:	White polar bear or substitute
Tail:	Golden pheasant crest dyed purple	Cheeks:	Jungle cock
Body:	Dark red seal fur or substitute	Head:	Claret
Collar:	Purple hackle		

Dave McNeese of Salem, Oregon, accidentally originated the "Mistake" around 1988 when he confused the dressing of the Surgeon General, which he was tying for his shop. By the time he discovered his error he had tied several dozen flies and decided to put them out for sale anyway. Since then, the popularity of Dave's Mistake has grown steadily and the fly continues to take steelhead throughout the Northwest.

Tied by John Shewey

Tied by Greased Line Fly Shoppe

DEAN RIVER LANTERN

Tail:	Black squirrel tail, the length of the body	Body:	Red, yellow or orange Edge-Brite
		Collar:	Red, yellow or orange hackle

Originally the body of this fly was constructed by wrapping flat monofilament over floss over silver tinsel. According to Bob Wagoner, a professional fly tier from Lewiston, Idaho, who is responsible for popularizing the Lanterns, the style was introduced by Dr. Arthur Cohen from San Francisco, California, who also discovered Edge-Brite, and applied it to this fly.

Tied by Bruce McNae

DEAN SPADE

Tag:	Flat silver tinsel	Body:	Black seal fur or substitute, picked out
Butt:	Rusty orange or bright green dubbing		
		Collar:	Grizzly hackle

This fly was developed by Bruce McNae in 1988 during a trip he made to the Dean River with Trey Combs, while Combs was researching a chapter on the Dean for his book *Steelhead Fly Fishing*. McNae, who is the president of the Washington Steelhead Flyfishers and a trustee of the Deer Creek Restoration Fund, says that it fishes best on a floating line, just below the surface.

Tied by Walt Johnson

DEEP PURPLE SPEY

Body:	Deep purple mohair		tinsel
Rib:	Flat silver tinsel	Collar:	Long, soft hackle dyed deep purple
Hackle:	Dark brown ringneck pheasant rump feather, folded and palmered forward from the second turn of	Wing:	A pair of red golden pheasant body feathers tied low over the body

Steelhead fly-fishing pioneer Walt Johnson of Arlington, Washington, who credits Ken McLeod for introducing purple into steelhead flies as early as the 1930s and 40s, came up with this Spey pattern. Johnson also experimented successfully with the use of purple, but credits his friend the late Syd Glasso for inspiring the creation of the Deep Purple Spey which has proven tremendously effective.

Tied by Farrow Allen

DEER CREEK

Tail:	Red hackle barbs	Throat:	Purple marabou, slightly shorter than the wing
Body:	Flat silver tinsel		
Rib:	Oval silver tinsel	Collar:	Soft and webby Silver Doctor blue hackle
Wing:	Purple marabou		

The Deer Creek is a straightforward marabou pattern, originated by Bob Arnold for winter steelheading in Washington, that's usually fished on a sinking line, quartered either down or upstream - whatever it takes to get the fly to winter fish holding deep and tight to the bottom.

DEL COOPER

Tag:	Flat silver tinsel	Rib:	Fine silver tinsel
Tail:	Red hackle barbs	Collar:	Red hackle
Body:	Purple wool	Wing:	White bucktail

An early purple fly that was designed by Mike Kennedy from Lake Oswego, Oregon. It has grown in popularity in recent years, especially in Oregon's Willamette River drainage where purple is almost a prerequisite for a successful fly pattern.

Tied by Mike McCoy

DEMON, GOLDEN

Tail:	Golden pheasant crest or yellow hackle barbs	Wing:	Bronze mallard, brown bucktail, or red squirrel tail
Body:	Oval gold tinsel	Cheeks:	Jungle cock (optional)
Throat:	Orange hackle as a collar, pulled down and back	Head:	Red

The origin of the Golden Demon is confusing because the paths of its development appear to come from many directions. The clearest route is from New Zealand and a Golden Demon streamer fly that Zane Grey or Fred Burnham brought into the country during the mid-1930s, and fished successfully on the Rogue River for steelhead. Variations of the Golden Demon have been developed for trout and Atlantic salmon also.

Tied by Joe Howell

DEPENDABLE, BLUE

Hook:	8X long streamer	Hackle:	Large gray mallard body feather palmered from the second turn of tinsel, followed by a large palmered plume of teal blue marabou
Tag:	Flat silver tinsel		
Tail:	Golden pheasant breast feathers, tied flat on top		
Body:	Rear ⅓: Black leech yarn Front ⅔: Blue leech yarn	Throat:	Several turns of black marabou followed by barred teal
Rib:	Flat and oval silver tinsel	Wing:	Strips of dark turkey tail

This is one in a series of winter flies originated by Joe Rossano of Seattle who was influenced by the 19th century Scottish Dee Eagles. Rossano rarely ties them smaller than size 2, and he fishes them successfully in high water. The profile of these flies is maintained by the palmered mallard-body feather that supports the marabou and keeps it from clinging against the body.

Tied by Joe Rossano

DESCHUTES MADNESS

Tag:	Flat gold tinsel and fluorescent red floss	Collar:	Purple hackle
		Wing:	Purple polar bear hair or substitute over which are strands of purple crystal flash
Tail:	Strands of fluorescent red floss		
Body:	Purple crystal chenille palmered over fluorescent red floss		

When cellophane and crystal chenilles became available, Dave McNeese, John Shewey and Bill Schiffman began experimenting with these new materials and developed a series of fly patterns they referred to as The Madness Series. This is one of the best and has met with tremendous success on the Deschutes River. The Marabou Madness is another excellent pattern that substitutes purple marabou for the hair wing.

Tied by John Shewey

Tied by Austin McWithey

DILLON CREEK SPECIAL

Tail:	Guinea fowl hackle barbs over which are 4 strands of gold crystal flash	Rib:	Flat silver tinsel
		Wing:	Golden badger hackle tips, curving outward
Butt:	Fluorescent red chenille	Collar:	Guinea fowl
Body:	Black chenille	Head:	Red

The Dillon Creek Special was originated in 1989 by Austin McWithey, of Happy Camp, California, for the prevailing low-water conditions on the Lower Klamath River. This is the winter version; a summer variation is dressed with a chartreuse butt, gold tinsel, gold crystal flash horns and a sparse beard of guinea fowl barbs.

Tied by Al Doll

DOLL'S STEELHEAD SPRUCE

Hook:	3x long		which is black marabou about half as long as the badger
Body:	Red wool		
Wing:	A pair of light badger hackles over	Collar:	Light badger hackle, tied full

Al Doll of Lansing, Michigan, developed this variation of the Spruce streamer and originally tied it in the style of a Matuka. Commercial tiers found it easier to tie a conventional wing and modified the dressing to this form. An effective pattern when steelhead are fresh and have not yet settled into lies.

Tied by Tim Coleman

DRAIN'S 20

Tip:	Flat silver tinsel and yellow fluorescent floss	Throat:	Purple hackle
		Wing:	Two golden pheasant rump feathers dyed red (cock-of-the rock substitute) over which is gray squirrel tail
Tail:	Golden pheasant tippet and a golden-yellow toucan substitute		
Body:	Fluorescent red floss		
Rib:	Flat silver tinsel	Cheeks:	Jungle cock

This beautiful pattern was originated by Wes Drain of Seattle, Washington, and was named the "Drain 20" after he took a twenty-pound, seven-ounce steelhead on the Skagit River, setting a Washington State record that held for nearly twenty years.

Tied by Mark Noble

EGG SUCKING LEECH

Hook:	3X or 4X long	Head:	A ball (egg) of fluorescent chenille, usually red, orange, pink or green
Tail:	Black marabou		
Body:	Black chenille	Note:	This fly is commonly weighted and is tied in many color combinations
Hackle:	Soft black, hackle tied in by the tip and palmered forward		

Despite its strange name the Egg Sucking Leech is an excellent pattern that seems to have originated in Alaska. It was designed for fishing deep on a sinking line, dead drifted along the bottom and then allowed to swing up at the end of the drift as the line tightens. The fly has been a great success and its use has spread throughout steelhead country.

EGG SUCKING LEECH, LEAD EYE

Hook:	3x long	Hackle:	Soft black, tied in by the tip and palmered forward
Tail:	Several strands of pearl crystal flash over which is a strip of black rabbit fur	Head:	Chrome lead eyes and fluorescent red-orange chenille
Body:	Black sparkle chenille	Head:	Fluorescent orange

This fast-sinking variation of the Egg Sucking Leech was developed by Joe Howell. It is a good winter pattern that displays a touch of hot color, flash at the head and has greater potential for a deeper presentation in fast water. Also tied with a fluorescent-green head and a green crystal-flash tail for highly discolored water.

Tied by Joe Howell

ELECTRIC BLUE

Body:	Flat gold tinsel		of pearl crystal flash
Rib:	Oval silver tinsel	Collar:	Red followed by shorter purple hackle
Wing:	Royal blue marabou, wound like a collar, over which are a few strands		

West Coast steelheader Sean Gallagher originated this bright marabou wet fly for winter steelheading. The combination of royal-blue marabou flanked by the red and purple hackle offers an exciting appearance to this pattern that is usually presented on a sinking line.

Tied by Bob Aid

ENCHANTRESS

Tail:	Soft red hackle barbs	Hackle:	Gray Spey hackle, palmered forward from the first turn of tinsel
Butt:	Green fur		
Body	Black fur	Wing:	White goose shoulder, tied tent-like and low over the body
Rib:	Flat gold tinsel		

The Enchantress was originated by Roger Turner of Burnaby, British Columbia. Roger is a devoted steelhead angler who, with his wife Grace, operates Turner's Fly Shop in Vancouver. This is one of his favorite wet flies for the Dean River, but it also fishes well on most other rivers in the province.

Tied by Roger Turner

ESTAZ WOOLY

Tail:	Yellow bucktail over which is pearlescent yellow crystal flash	Rib:	Counter-wrapped fluorescent red thread, securing the hackle without mashing down the Estaz
Body:	Red Estaz chenille		
Hackle:	Palmered yellow	Collar:	Mallard flank

This pattern is a variation of Joe Butorac's Steel Woolie (which see) that effectively utilizes some of the new synthetic fly-tying materials. It can be tied in any color combinations you fancy.

Tied by Kaufmann's Streamborn

FALL FAVORITE

Body: Flat or embossed silver tinsel
Collar: Red hackle
Wing: Fluorescent orange bucktail, calftail

or polar bear
Head: Red or black

Tied by Dick Stewart

Introduced by Lloyd Silvius for fall- and winter-run fish on the Eel River around 1946, the Fall Favorite is considered a standard from autumn through early winter. Variations include a fluorescent-orange marabou wing, a Matuka-style wing, or a streamer-hackle wing. It is commonly dressed with all-fluorescent material for winter fish and continues to be very popular from California to Alaska.

FARRAR MARABOU

Body: Purple dubbing
Rib: Flat silver tinsel
Hackle: Purple marabou fibers, stripped from the stem and placed in a dubbing loop with the short butt ends trimmed; the loop is twisted to lock in the fibers which are stroked to the rear with moistened

fingers as they are wrapped around the hook like hackle
Wing: Purple Flashabou
Collar: Red golden pheasant body feather followed by teal
Topping: The tip of a golden pheasant body feather

Tied by Garry Stewart

Marabou flies are an important tool for the winter steelhead angler. Seattle guide and fly tier John Farrar, inspired by Poul Jorgensen's method of dubbing rabbit fur as hackle by means of a dubbing loop, adapted this original technique for applying marabou.

FERRY CANYON

Tail: Purple hackle barbs
Body: Rear ¼: Fluorescent red-orange yarn
          Front ¾: Purple chenille
Rib: Fine oval silver tinsel

Wing: Strands of red, blue, wine and pearl crystal flash over which is purple marabou
Collar: Purple hackle

Tied by Dick Stewart

Randall Kaufmann of Portland, Oregon, and Kaufmann's Streamborn Flies developed this appealing dark-purple marabou fly with a spot of bright fluorescence and a little flash. It was named for the boulder-strewn runs of the Ferry Canyon section of the Deschutes River where this fly produces well in the early season, and seems to be most effective when visibility is poor.

FIREFLY

Hook: Gold Eagle Claw #1197 G
Tail: Fluorescent orange hackle barbs
Body: Fluorescent orange chenille
Rib: Flat silver tinsel

Collar: Fluorescent orange hackle
Wing: White polar bear or substitute over which is white marabou
Cheeks: Jungle cock

Tied by Bill Yonge

The Firefly was first tied by Bill Yonge of Vancouver, British Columbia, in the late 1960s for the Squamish River system. Originally tied with a marabou wing only, Yonge found that the marabou fouled easily, by getting wrapped around the hook. He addressed this problem by including an underwing of stiff hair. It has proven itself a steady producer on rivers in British Columbia for winter-run fish.

FLAT CAR

Tail:	Black hackle barbs	Collar:	Black hackle
Butt:	Fluorescent green yarn	Wing:	A few strands of black and pearl
Body:	Black chenille		crystal flash over which is black
Rib:	Fine oval silver tinsel		marabou

The Flat Car, introduced in 1989 by Randall Kaufmann, is a variation of the Green Butt Skunk. It is most effective for fishing at dusk since the fly is highly visible due to its bulky silhouette, and the fluorescent green is prominent in the fading light.

Tied by Dick Stewart

FORRESTER

Tail:	Orange-yellow calftail	Throat:	Orange-yellow calftail
Body:	Rear ⅔: Fluorescent orange che-nille	Wing:	Orange-yellow calftail
		Head:	Red
	Front ⅓: Black chenille		

This popular pattern was developed by George Richey in 1979 and named for Claude Forrester of the Backcast Fly Shop in Benzonia, Michigan. It is a good attractor fly in the spring.

Tied by George Richey

FRAMMUS

Body:	Fluorescent chartreuse chenille	Wing:	Fluorescent cerise Glo-Bug yarn

Although not classified as an egg pattern, the Frammus wet-fly pattern is pretty much the same as the Bright Roe egg pattern (which see), which seems to have developed as a salmon fly in Alaska. Both patterns have proved highly effective in British Columbia for steelhead as well as for winter fishing on the rivers of Lake Onatario.

Tied by Fran Verdoliva

FRANK'S FLY

Body:	Fluorescent orange chenille	Wing:	White calftail
Hackle:	Fluorescent orange, palmered over the body	Head:	Fluorescent red

Frank's Fly is a an effective design that appears to be a cross between a Polar Shrimp and an orange Wooly Worm. It was originated by Frank Moore of Anchorage, Alaska, and is fished deep like a nymph, drifted naturally along the bottom and finally retrieved with short jerks. It is an excellent pattern on Kodiak Island and should be an effective winter pattern on any steelhead river.

Tied by Dick Stewart

Tied by Dick Stewart

FREIGHT TRAIN, KRYSTAL FLASH

Tail:	Purple hackle barbs	Rib:	Fine oval silver tinsel
Body:	Rear ¼: Fluorescent red-orange floss	Collar:	Purple hackle
	Second ¼: Fluorescent red floss	Wing:	Blue Krystal Flash over which is pearl Krystal Flash
	Front ½: Black chenille		

The Freight Train was originated by Randall Kaufmann, of Portland, Oregon. It evolved from the late 1970s and through the early 1980s when he was operating fly-fishing schools on the Deschutes River. The original Freight Train had a simple white calftail wing. This was superceded by the Flashabou Freight Train, which then evolved into this variation. It is among the top-10 flies sold at Kaufmann's Streamborn Fly Fishing Shops.

Tied by Gary Selig

GARY'S ASSASSIN

Tail:	Black Arctic fox tail hair, about 1 ½ times the length of the body	Body:	Fluorescent green yarn
		Collar:	Soft natural black hackle
Tag:	Fluorescent red thread	Head:	Fluorescent red

Introduced as a steelhead pattern around 1988 by commercial fly tier Gary Selig of Mertztown, Pennsylvania. Selig first discovered this fly in Quebec where it was being fished for trout. He later modified it for steelhead and began fishing it on the tributaries of Lake Ontario. It has been very effective during the fall in small sizes and during the spring in larger sizes.

Tied by Gary Selig

GARY'S SMURF

Hook:	Short shank or egg type hook	Collar:	Grizzly hackle
Tail:	Fine black hair	Eyes:	Small silver bead chain
Body:	None		

This is a recent addition to the flies designed by Gary Selig and it has proved a killing pattern in Pulaski, New York, on the Salmon River as well as the Grindstone and North and South Sandy Creeks. It's most effective in small sizes cast across and downstream to spooky, heavily-fished steelhead.

Tied by Patrick's Fly Shop

GIANT KILLER

Tail:	Purple hackle barbs	Throat:	Purple hackle, long
Body:	Fluorescent green floss	Wing:	White polar bear or substitute

The Giant Killer was designed by Don Larson, of Seattle, and has been fished successfully on the Kispiox River and the Skeena River system in British Columbia. The fly is dressed very sparsely, and was a favorite of the late Roy Patrick, who opened Seattle's first fly-fishing shop.

GLADIATOR

Tail:	Scarlet hackle barbs	Collar:	Grizzly hackle
Body:	Green floss	Wing:	Gray squirrel tail
Rib:	Peacock herl		

This fly was originated for summer steelheading on the Klickitat and Kispiox in the 1960s by octogenarian Nick Gayeski, a Washington State steelheader for over 50 years. Although it is not a widely known pattern, between Gayeski, his son and fishing companions, the Gladiator has accounted for many steelhead throughout the years.

Tied by Tim Coleman

GOLD HERON

Body:	Rear ⅔: Flat gold tinsel		palmered from the third turn of
	Front ⅓: Orange seal or substitute		hackle
Rib:	Oval gold tinsel	Throat:	Widgeon flank fibers
Hackle:	Grey heron substitute with one	Wing:	Widgeon flank
	side stripped of hackle barbs and	Head:	Orange

The Gold Heron was originated by the late Syd Glasso of Forks, Washington, for winter steelheading on the rivers of the Olympic Peninsula.

Tied by Bob Veverka

GOLDEN EDGE ORANGE

Tag:	Flat silver tinsel		is bronze mallard
Tail:	Golden pheasant crest	Topping:	Golden pheasant crest
Body:	Orange dubbing	Cheeks:	Jungle cock (optional)
Rib:	Flat silver tinsel	Head:	Orange
Throat:	Guinea fowl barbs, beard style	Note:	Also tied as a Golden Edge Yellow
Wing:	Sparse gray squirrel tail over which		with a yellow body and head.

This favorite wet fly, dating back to 1971, was designed by Harry Lemire of Black Diamond, Washington. This and the Golden Edge Yellow are two of Lemire's favorite wet-fly patterns. He suggests using small sizes on a greased line in the summer, and large sizes on a wet line during the winter.

Tied by Harry Lemire

GOLDEN GIRL

Tail:	Orange hackle barbs		flanked by a pair of golden pheas-
Body:	Flat gold tinsel		ant tippet feathers
Wing:	Orange polar bear or substitute	Collar:	Orange hackle

The Golden Girl is a simple, bright featherwing pattern for winter-run fish. It was introduced by Roderick Haig-Brown in the 1940s for the Campbell River on Vancouver Island in British Columbia.

Tied by John Olschewsky

Tied by Steve Petit

GREEN BUTT

Tag:	Fluorescent green floss	Throat:	Black hackle
Body:	Black fur dubbing	Wing:	Red squirrel tail
Rib:	Fine flat silver tinsel		

A simple, dark pattern with a bright spot of color at the rear, the Green Butt seems to have evolved from the well-known Atlantic-salmon fly from New Brunswick, the Black Bear, Green Butt.

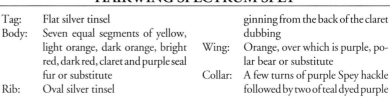

HAIRWING SPECTRUM SPEY

Tag:	Flat silver tinsel		ginning from the back of the claret dubbing
Body:	Seven equal segments of yellow, light orange, dark orange, bright red, dark red, claret and purple seal fur or substitute	Wing:	Orange, over which is purple, polar bear or substitute
Rib:	Oval silver tinsel	Collar:	A few turns of purple Spey hackle followed by two of teal dyed purple
Hackle:	Palmered black Spey hackle, be-	Head:	Pale gray

After reading the dressing it is evident how this pattern, which was originated by John Shewey of Aumsville, Oregon, was given its name. Shewey, an avid steelheader and a regular on the North Santiam, declares "The idea . . . is simply to present a range of colors to the fish . . . and let the fish see the color that it wants to see."

Tied by John Shewey

HERNIATOR

Body:	Peacock colored Poly Flash (Paxton's Peacock Astro)	Wing:	Peacock Poly Flash, picked apart
		Collar:	Guinea fowl, one or two turns
Thorax:	Peacock herl		

This pattern was originated by Californian Bill Geise for the Klamath and Trinity Rivers, where it is a very effective fly. It was named the Herniator because the day after it was introduced Geise was admitted to the hospital with a hernia that he claims was due to the strain of catching so many steelhead on the new fly.

Tied by Fred Contaoi

HIGHTIDE

Tag:	Flat gold tinsel		and palmered over the dubbed fur
Tail:	Orange golden pheasant	Throat:	Barred teal dyed orange
Butt:	Black ostrich	Wing:	A pair of barred flank feathers from a hen pheasant, dyed orange
Body:	Three turns of golden-orange silk followed by blended orange and red seal fur or substitute	Cheeks:	Orange dyed hen hackle as a substitute for cock-of-the-rock
Rib:	Flat and oval gold tinsel	Topping:	Orange golden pheasant crest
Hackle:	Pheasant body feather dyed orange	Head:	Red

The Hightide was originated by Mark Waslick, a gifted young fly tier from Middlebury, Vermont, who dressed this pattern for British Columbia where it has proven very effective on the Dean and Babine Rivers. Although an easterner, Waslick has spent considerable time in Washington and Oregon with west coast fly tiers.

Tied by Mark Waslick

HIT MAN

Tail: Dark blue Flashabou
Body: Purple Mylar Poly Flash or Diamond Braid
Wing: Black marabou over which are several strands of dark blue Flashabou
Collar: Soft black hackle

Head: Black with a couple of strands of dark blue Flashabou wrapped at the back of the head and whip-finished on top with the butt ends left long extending over the top of the wing

The Hit Man, also known as the Dean River Special, is an effective pattern designed by Mark Noble for the wild rivers of British Columbia. Fished in a variety of sizes, its popularity on the rivers in southwestern Washington has steadily grown since its introduction in 1986.

Tied by Mark Noble

HORRIBLE MATUKA

Body: Fluorescent pink chenille
Rib: Oval silver tinsel
Wing: Two to four badger hackles dyed fluorescent orange and tied onto

the body Matuka style
Collar: Badger hackle dyed fluorescent orange

The Horrible Matuka pattern was devised by the late Harry Darbee, of Livingston Manor, New York, for his annual fall trip to the Margaree River in Nova Scotia where the Atlantic salmon are notably susceptible to large, bright streamers. At some point the pattern was introduced for steelhead fishing and it proved to be an instant success. The Matuka style, with the wing secured to the fly body, maintains the wing feathers in a fixed position.

Tied by Dick Stewart

IAN'S SILVER SPEY

Body: Flat silver tinsel
Hackle: Webby black Spey-type hackle, palmered over the body

Rib: Oval gold tinsel
Collar: Guinea fowl
Wing: Bronze mallard

Tied in 1987 by Canadian guide and fly dresser Ian James of Balmoral Feathers in Guelph, Ontario, this fly is most effective on bright days when the water is slightly off-color. Although Spey flies are popular among west coast steelheaders, it is rare to find them in use on the rivers of the Great Lakes. James and his clients, however, frequently use them with good success.

Tied by Ian James

ICEBERG

Tail: Red hackle barbs
Body: Pearl crystal chenille
Rib: Flat silver tinsel

Collar: Blue hackle
Wing: Gray squirrel tail dyed blue

The Iceberg was originally designed for the Deschutes River by Keith Stonebreaker of Lewistown, Idaho. Blue steelhead flies are rare and the Iceberg as an alternative pattern has shown increasing popularity on the inland steelhead rivers of Idaho.

Tied by Dick Stewart

Tied by Alec Jackson

Tied by Kent Bulfinch

Tied by Wayne Orzel

Tied by Dick Stewart

JACOB'S COAT

Tail:	Extremely fine deer body hair		around the hook shank
Body:	A mixture of ostrich, dyed various colors (red, purple, yellow, etc.) and peacock herl twisted onto fine oval gold tinsel and wrapped	Collar:	Orange or mixed red and yellow soft hackle
		Head:	Fluorescent red

The multicolored Jacob's Coat was originated by Alec Jackson of Kenmore, Washington, primarily for fishing inland and east of the Cascades. It's effective when fished using a greased-line technique during the summer and into the fall, through mid-November.

JUICY BUG

Hook:	Usually a small double	Rib:	Oval or flat silver tinsel
Tail:	Dyed red hackle barbs or hair	Wing:	White bucktail, divided and set upright
Butt:	Black chenille		
Body:	Red chenille	Cheek:	Jungle cock

The Juicy Bug was originated for the Rogue River by Ike Tower and Bob Chandler, a pair of Rogue River regulars from Coos Bay, Oregon. They designed their fly to be durable, with the look of the Royal Coachman, a popular but extremely fragile fly. It is dressed in the typical Rogue River style with its divided, cocked wing, and should be fished with short strips of the line.

KALAMA SPECIAL

Tail:	Red hackle barbs		palmered forward over the body with several additional turns taken at the throat
Body:	Yellow (original) or fluorescent yellow chenille or yarn		
Hackle:	Badger hackle tied in by the tip,	Wing:	White bucktail or calftail

Originally tied by Mooch Abrams of Portland, Oregon, this fly was first tied for sea-run cutthroat trout, and popularized by Mike Kennedy in the 1930s and 40s on Washington's Kalama River for summer-run steelhead. It is still a good fly on many rivers and is most popular during the late-summer months when grasshoppers are abundant. The Kalama Special is sometimes referred to as the Kennedy Special. Abrams is also credited with introducing the "double-haul" cast in the 1930s.

KALEIDOSCOPE

Tail:	Red hackle barbs		together
Body:	Pearl Flashabou over a foundation of purple floss	Wing:	White calftail over which are strands of blue and purple Flashabou
Collar:	Blue and purple hackle wound		

The Kaleidoscope was originated by Walt Balek of the Inland Empire Fly Fishing Club in Spokane, Washington. The pattern works well in fall as winter approaches and water temperatures start to drop. The body of this fly appears luminous in dark water or on overcast days when tied with a thin layer of Flashabou.

KINGFISHER BLUE SPEY

Tail:	Blue Amherst pheasant tippets
Body:	Light blue floss
Rib:	Flat silver tinsel
Hackle:	Palmered, white, black-tipped Spey hackle
Wing:	White over which are blue hen hackle tips
Throat:	Several turns of light blue hen hackle over which are strands of silver pheasant body feather fibers
Cheeks:	Brown kingfisher back feather
Topping:	Dark blue-black Amherst pheasant crest
Head:	White

Tied by Walt Johnson

This recent pattern from Walt Johnson of Arlington, Washington, was designed for the milky-blue rivers that result from glacial melt. Born in Kirkland in 1915 he grew up along the eastern shores of Lake Washington where he developed his love for the sport of fishing. Over the years Johnson has made a significant contribution to steelhead fly-fishing.

KISPIOX BRIGHT

Tail:	Red calftail mixed with a few strands of yellow crystal flash
Body:	Purple chenille
Rib:	Flat silver tinsel
Collar:	Fluorescent orange hackle
Wing:	White bucktail over which is yellow bucktail mixed with a few strands of yellow crystal flash (synthetic hair is sometimes substituted for bucktail)

Tied by Dick Stewart

This bright fly was designed by Bob York for high, but relatively-clear water conditions on British Columbia's Kispiox River. In off-color water York prefers a dark pattern like his Kispiox Dark that has a green floss body and black hair and crystal flash wing. York fishes salmon commercially in the summer and spends the balance of his time fishing steelhead, from Alaska to southern Oregon.

KISPIOX SPECIAL

Tail:	Red hair
Body:	Fluorescent orange chenille or wool
Collar:	Red hackle, applied before the wing
Wing:	White hair

Tied by Farrow Allen

In 1957, Karl Mausser and Roy Pitts collaborated to invent a new pattern that would attract the legendary fish of the Kispiox River in British Columbia. In October of 1962, Mausser beached a fly-record steelhead of 33 pounds in the Kispiox River on a Kispiox Special. The fly was named by Drew Wookey who owned the fishing lodge on the Kispiox where Mausser stayed while fishing. This fly is very similar to the popular Polar Shrimp (which see).

KNUDSEN'S SPIDER

Tail:	Mallard flank barbs, long
Body:	Yellow chenille
Collar:	About two turns of folded grizzly hackle, in front of which are about four turns of folded mallard flank feather

Tied by Russ Miller

During the 1930s Al Knudsen of Everett, Washington, pioneered the use of wet spiders for steelhead fishing. Trout-fly spiders date back to the 15th century, but their use for steelhead fishing can be directly credited to Knudsen and a handful of his followers.

Tied by Bob Borden

KRYSTAL BULLET, BLACK

Tail:	Red Krystal Flash	Bullet-head and hackle:	Black Krystal Flash
Body:	Black chenille, one turn taken under the tail		tied down with red or fluorescent green thread

This example is just one of a series of Krystal Bullets that are tied in as many color combinations as there are colors of material. The Krystal Bullets, originated by Bob Borden, owner of Hareline Dubbin of Monroe, Oregon, have been one of the most consistent producers of winter steelhead since their recent introduction.

Tied by Mike McCoy

LADY CAROLINE

Tail:	Red golden pheasant breast feather barbs	Throat:	Red golden pheasant breast feather barbs
Body:	Two parts olive and one part brown seal fur or substitute, blended	Wing:	Bronze mallard
Rib:	Oval silver tinsel	Head:	Claret thread

The Lady Caroline is a variation of the ancient Scottish Spey pattern that has been modified and simplified for steelhead fishing. This somber fly is effective in low water for summer and fall fishing.

Tied by Walt Johnson

LADY COACHMAN

Tag:	Flat silver tinsel and cerise floss over silver tinsel	Collar:	Soft hackle dyed fluorescent pink
Tail:	Cerise hackle barbs	Wing:	Fine white bucktail or a similar fine white hair like rabbit or fox
Body:	Peacock herl, then fluorescent pink yarn, then peacock herl	Cheeks:	Kingfisher or substitute
		Topping:	Golden pheasant crest

The Lady Coachman was derived from the popular Royal Coachman by Walt Johnson of Arlington, Washington, in the 1950s for use on the North Fork of the Stillaguamish River. A summer-run pattern, it is particularly useful in fading light as the pinks in this fly appear radiant at dusk.

Tied by Russ Miller

LADY KAREN

Tag:	Flat silver tinsel		ward over the front half of the body
Tail:	Red hackle barbs, short		
Body:	Black seal fur or substitute	Wing:	Black marabou
Rib:	Oval silver tinsel	Collar:	Green wing teal breast feather
Hackle:	Black Spey hackle palmered for-		

The Lady Karen was originated in 1975 by Russ Miller of Arlington, Washington, for high-water conditions on the North Fork of the Stillaguamish. Several tributaries of the North Fork contain clay banks that discolor the river during periods of extended rain, and the Lady Karen is highly visible in this type of off-color water. It was named for Karen Gobin who, like her husband Steve, is a fly dresser and angler from Marysville, Washington.

LEAD EYE LEECH

Tail:	Black rabbit strip		palmered forward
Body:	Black chenille	Head:	Chrome plated lead eyes and black
Rib:	Fine oval silver tinsel		chenille
Hackle:	Soft black , tied in by the tip and		

This leech variation was designed by Joe Howell of the Blue Heron Fly Shop for fishing the slots and deep runs that dominate the North Umpqua River. It is usually tied either all black or black with a purple or chartreeuse tail. Howell says that during the winter run a chartreuse-tail version seems to have the edge.

Tied by Joe Howell

MAGENTA SPIDER

Tag:	Green Flashabou		Mylar (optional)
Tail:	Sparse fluorescent yellow hackle barbs	Collar:	Fluorescent yellow hackle followed by folded (doubled) mallard
Body:	Magenta chenille	Topping:	Sparse red, orange or pink polar
Wing:	A few strands of pearlescent		bear fur or substitute

The Magenta Spider was originated by Bob Betzig, Sr. of Snohomish, Washington, in the 1960s and was inspired by the Spider dressings of Al Knudsen. It is fished primarily for summer steelhead in a wide range of sizes depending on river conditions. Over the years the influnce of Al Knudsen can be seen in the flies of both Betzig and his friend Walt Johnson.

Tied by Bob Betzig

MARCH BROWN

Tag:	Flat gold tinsel	Throat:	Partridge hackle
Tail:	Brown partridge body feather barbs	Wing:	Mottled turkey wing quill seg-
Body:	Hare's ear fur dubbing		ments
Rib:	Flat gold tinsel		

This is John Olschewsky's variation of an old British trout fly that has been successfully adapted to Atlantic-salmon fishing but is frequently overlooked in steelhead circles. It is an excellent fly during the summer when rivers run low and clear, the fish are spooky, and brightly colored flies are intrusive. Olschewsky suggests fishing it on a floating line, just below the surface.

Tied by John Olschewsky

MATARELLI SPECIAL

Wire foundation:	Loop of stiff twisted gold wire, tied in at the tail and extending along the sides of the hook shank to provide a flattened base		or substitute
		Collar:	Short gray (marabou) down, in front of which is a turn of irides-cent golden green neck hackle, in
Tail:	Badger hair, elevated by the wire		front of which is a longer blue-green peacock body feather
Body:	Woven tan and yellow poly yarn		

This unique, woven-body pattern was designed by Frank Matarelli of San Francisco, the inventor of many popular fly-tying tools. The tail position may be adjusted by changing the angle of the wire loop at the rear. Matarelli ties many variations in a multitude of colors. The significance of this fly rests in its design, not the specific materials shown here.

Tied by Frank Matarelli

Tied by Doug Stewart

MAX CANYON

Tail:	Orange and white calftail, mixed	Collar:	Black hackle
Body:	Rear ⅓: Orange wool	Wing:	Two parts white calf or bucktail
	Front ⅔: Black wool or dubbing		over which is one part orange
Rib:	Oval gold tinsel		

Developed in 1972 at Mack's Canyon on the Deschutes River, this pattern originated with Doug Stewart of Gresham, Oregon. Its name was intentionally misspelled to draw attention away from the already popular Mack's Canyon area. A variation known as the Dark Max Canyon was later developed by Larry Piatt of Pineville, Oregon, for overcast days or off-colored water. It is nearly the same as the original but substitutes black for the white calftail in the wing. (See also Stewart)

Tied by John Shewey

MAXWELL'S PURPLE MATUKA

Tag:	Flat silver tinsel		Matuka style
Body:	Black seal fur or substitute	Collar:	Purple hackle
Rib:	Oval silver tinsel	Head:	Gray
Wing:	Two broad purple hackles tied		

This fly was originated in the mid 1970s by Forrest Maxwell of Salem, Oregon. Purple seems to be the dominant color of flies originating in this area and Maxwell's very popular all-purple Matuka is no exception. This Matuka version is very effective locally on the North Santiam as well as the Clearwater, the Umpqua and McKenzie.

Tied by Skip Morris

McLEOD UGLY

| Tail: | Red fluff from the base of a hackle dyed red | Hackle: | Grizzly, tied in by the tip and palmered forward |
| Body: | Black chenille | Wing: | Black bear, bucktail or moose hair |

The McLeod Ugly was developed during the 1962 season by father and son steelheading notables, Ken and George McLeod of Seattle. Although the McLeod Ugly is a well-known dark pattern for fishing in Washington, it is, according to Ken, even more effective in British Columbia.

Tied by Farrow Allen

MICKEY FINN MARABOU

| Body: | Pearlescent or silver Mylar tubing attached at the butt with fluorescent red thread | | low marabou over which is red marabou followed by fluorescent yellow marabou |
| Wing: | Sparse bunches of fluorescent yel- | Head: | Fluorescent red |

This famous trout streamer has been be very useful for winter steelhead on Lake Ontario's Salmon River when dressed with marabou. It is usually cast upstream and allowed to sink, tumble downstream naturally and swim up to the surface at the end of the drift.

MIDNIGHT SUN

Tag: Flat silver tinsel
Tail: Orange hackle barbs
Body: Fluorescent orange floss over flat silver tinsel
Rib: Flat silver tinsel
Wing: White marabou to the end of the tail, over which is a shorter bunch of white marabou, over which is a shorter bunch of mixed orange and yellow marabou
Throat: Mixed orange and yellow marabou
Collar: Rose red hackle
Head: Fluorescent red

Tied by Trey Combs

The Midnight Sun was developed by west coast steelhead authority Trey Combs, author of *Steelhead Fly Fishing*, as a winter pattern for discolored water. It has also proved to be a good pattern for fishing in the high, off-color waters of spring, for fresh-run fish.

MIGRANT ORANGE

Tag: Copper tinsel and fluorescent orange floss over copper tinsel
Tail: Fluorescent orange hackle barbs or hair
Body: Fluorescent orange-red yarn
Rib: Flat copper tinsel
Collar: Soft orange hackle
Wing: Fluorescent orange acrylic hair or bucktail over which is a strand of fluorescent orange-red wool

Tied by Walt Johnson

In 1939 Walt Johnson took his first summer steelhead on a "crudely tied Orange Shrimp fly" that naturally became one of his favorite patterns. The Migrant Orange represents the culmination of years of experimentation and modification of that original orange fly. Johnson feels that this is "one of his most successful creations for summer and winter steelhead . . . that possesses the ability to move fish all season long."

MOONGLOW

Tag: Flat silver tinsel
Tail: Golden pheasant crest dyed magenta, on either side of which is a small (kingfisher) feather dyed violet
Body: Rear half: Flat silver tinsel, veiled top and bottom by pairs of (kingfisher) feathers dyed violet
Front half: Black ostrich herl, ribbed with fine oval silver tinsel
Hackle: Pheasant rump feather, dyed violet, palmered over the herl
Throat: Guinea fowl
Wing: A pair of black wing quills

Tied by Greg Scot Hunt

Greg Scot Hunt of Redmond, Washington, designed this attractive pattern for winter- and spring-run fish on the Skykomish and Sauk Rivers. Flies like this also evince the artistry which has been demonstrated in many modern steelhead fly designs.

MOVER

Tag: Oval gold tinsel
Body: Claret floss
Rib: Oval gold tinsel
Wing: Red squirrel tail
Collar: Natural lemon woodduck flank, followed by shorter guinea fowl dyed claret
Head: Claret

Tied by Tim Coleman

This was the first and most successful of the "Movers" series that was first tied in 1986 by Tim Coleman of Linwood, Washington. Originally tied for the North Fork of the Stillaguamish, the Mover, in Coleman's words is most effective ". . . on summer fish that are holed up in late fall."

Tied by Umpqua Feather Merchants

MUDDLER MINNOW

Tail:	Paired mottled turkey wing quill segments		over which is a pair of mottled turkey wing quills segments
Body:	Flat or embossed gold tinsel	Head:	Natural deer body hair spun and
Wing:	Brown calftail or gray squirrel tail		clipped to form a collar

Originated as a trout fly by Don Gapen, the Muddler Minnow has spawned a variety of steelhead flies with spun deer-hair heads that have been designed for skating, dredging and everything in between.

Tied by Kaufmann's Streamborn

MUDDLER, KRYSTAL FLASH

Body:	Black Diamond Braid or embossed gold tinsel	mottled brown wing of turkey, grouse or similar feather
Wing:	Sparse black squirrel tail and black Krystal Flash over which is a	Head and collar: Spun black deer body hair, clipped flat on the top and bottom

This is one variation of the Krystal Flash Muddler series that was designed by John Hazel, a guide and a manager for Kaufmann's Streamborn Fly Shop. It has become one of the most popular steelhead muddlers in the northwest. Purple and olive variations are frequently used.

Tied by Scott Ripley

MUDDLER, PURPLE

Tail:	Purple marabou	brown
Body:	Claret angora goat	Head and collar: One turn of red angora
Rib:	Fine oval gold tinsel	yarn in front of which is spun and
Wing:	Gray squirrel tail dyed purple-	clipped deer body hair dyed purple

This Muddler Minnow variation was designed by Scott Ripley of Tigard, Oregon, shortly after he moved from the east coast to the west coast in the early 1980s. It was developed for the Deschutes River and is fished either on or below the surface. When Muddlers are intended to be fished on the surface they are dressed with a fairly large head, while those intended to sink are tied with small, streamlined heads.

Tied by Farrow Allen

NIGHT DANCER

Tail:	Red hackle barbs	Collar:	Deep purple hackle
Body:	Black floss	Wing:	Black calftail or bucktail
Rib:	Flat silver tinsel		

The Night Dancer was first tied by Frank Amato of Amato Publications in Portland, Oregon. Amato is a devoted steelhead angler and publisher of *Flyfishing* magazine and several dozen books on fishing. Trey Combs in *Steelhead Fly Fishing* describes tying the Night Dancer in a variety of sizes and fishing it with good results from Oregon to British Columbia.

NITE OWL

Tail:	Yellow hackle barbs	Collar:	Orange hackle
Butt:	Red chenille	Wing:	White hair
Body:	Oval silver tinsel		

Tied by Dick Stewart

The Nite Owl was originated by Lloyd Silvius of Eureka, California, in 1930 for fall- and winter-run steelhead on California's Eel River. This fly was one of the early hairwing steelhead patterns from one of the best-known fly tiers on the West Coast.

NIX'S WOOLLY SPECIAL

Body: Rear ½: Fluorescent chartreuse chenille
Front ½: Fluorescent pink che-nille
Hackle: Grizzly, palmered over the entire body

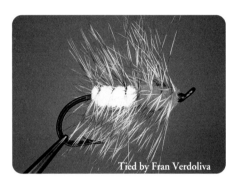
Tied by Fran Verdoliva

This Wooly Worm variation utilizes the same successful colors as the Frammus (which see). It is a favorite fly of Ron Nix, one of western New York's pioneer steelheaders on the Salmon River. It is used mostly in the spring when fish are on their beds and responding aggressively to the fly.

NOLA'S PINK SPEY

Tag:	Flat or oval silver tinsel		the neck of a ruffed grouse
Body:	Pink Glo-Bug yarn	Wing:	A pair of goose wing quill segments dyed pink
Rib:	Oval silver tinsel		
Collar:	A soft webby black feather from		

Tied by Tim Krahe

This moderately-bright Spey fly was introduced in 1979 by Tim Krahe of Manistee, Michigan, for winter steelhead. Named for his wife, this pattern is particularly effective in clear water on bright, sunny days.

OPTIC, BLACK

Body:	Oval gold (or silver) tinsel tied well down into the bend of the hook	Head:	Split brass bead clamped in at the head of the hook, painted black with a white iris and black pupil
Hackle:	Black		
Wing:	Black bucktail		

Tied by Mike McCoy

The uniquely designed Optic flies were originated by C. Jim Pray of Eureka, California, in the early 1940s. These fast-sinking, "bug-eyed" flies were intended for winter fishing on northern California's Eel River and they are tied in a variety of colors, both natural and fluorescent.

Tied by John Shewey

Tied by Bob Veverka

Tied by Marty Sherman

Tied by Bill McMillan

ORANGE EGRET SPEY

Tag:	Flat silver tinsel	Hackle:	One pale and one bright orange
Body:	First ¼: Orange floss		Spey hackle palmered over the or-
	Second ¼: Fluorescent red floss		ange dubbing
	Front ½: Bright orange seal fur or	Wing:	One or two pair of fluorescent red
	substitute		hackle tips
Rib:	Fine silver wire over the rear half	Collar:	Dark orange hackle
	and oval silver tinsel over the front	Head:	Red

This bright fly was designed for the coastal rivers of Oregon and Washington by John Shewey of Aumsville, Oregon. The Spey hackles for this pattern are carefully selected pheasant-rump feathers that have been bleached and dyed, in this case orange with black tips.

ORANGE HERON

Body:	Rear ⅔: Orange floss		heron
	Foward ⅓: Orange seal fur	Throat:	Teal flank (optional)
Rib:	Flat silver tinsel followed by fine	Wing:	Four short fluorescent orange
	oval silver tinsel		hackle tips, set low
Hackle:	Gray Spey hackle substitute for	Head:	Red

The Orange Heron may be the best known creation of the late Syd Glasso whose legendary flies are among the most beautiful ever tied for steelhead fishing. Before retiring to Seattle, Glasso was a high-school teacher in Forks, Washington. There he spent most of his free time perfecting his phenomenal skill as a fly tier and fishing the many rivers of the Olympic Peninsula.

OTTER BAR PURPLE

Tail:	Purple hackle barbs	Wing:	Red-brown ringneck pheasant
Tag:	Flat silver tinsel		body feather barbs
Body:	Purple yarn	Collar:	Purple hackle
Rib:	Flat silver	Head:	Claret

Marty Sherman, Editor of *Flyfishing* magazine, originated this purple pattern in 1986 while on a trip with his wife Joyce to the Salmon River in northern California. The fly was named after the camp at which they were staying, the Otter Bar Lodge.

PAINT BRUSH

Body:	Flat gold tinsel		quoise hackle
Body hackle:	Red-orange	Head:	Red
Collar:	Purple, in front of which is tur-		

This winter pattern was developed by Bill McMillan in 1973 and should not be confused with an older fly of the same name by Peter Schwab. McMillan named his fly after a wildflower, the indian paint brush. He once described it as "…a very simple fly that possessed a great deal of glowing movement." He suggests fishing it on a "floating line and strictly on a deep, natural drift."

PATRICIA

Tag:	Fine oval gold tinsel (optional)	Collar:	Claret hackle
Tail:	Claret hackle barbs	Wing:	White polar bear or substitute
Body:	Claret seal fur or substitute	Cheeks:	Jungle cock (optional)
Rib:	Oval gold tinsel	Head:	Claret

The Patricia was first tied for the Deschutes River in 1985. Its originator, Randy Stetzer, believes that claret is a color long overlooked by steelhead anglers. He has always preferred to fish with dark patterns in both clear and dirty water. He believes that dark flies don't spook fish in clear water and that the dark fly offers a stronger silhouette in discolored water.

Tied by Randy Stetzer

PERKINS #1

Butt:	Oval silver tinsel, long		between the two body halves
Tail:	Orange polar bear or substitute	Throat:	Mallard flank dyed black
Body:	Rear ½: Dubbed blue silk floss	Wing:	Two ringneck pheasant rump
	Front ½: Dubbed purple silk floss		feathers, dyed black and tied flat,
	(floss is cut in pieces, blended,		over which is a shorter natural or
	placed in a dubbing loop and		dyed pale green body feather
	wound on)	Sides:	Two golden pheasant crest feath-
Joint:	A turn of golden pheasant crest		ers curving around the wing

This pattern was originated by Kevin Perkins of Everett, Washington, for winter fishing. The flat wing tends to deflect water down, causing the long, supple fibers of the dubbed floss to move responsively in the current. It's a good winter fly on the Skagit and Skykomish Rivers.

Tied by Kevin Perkins

PETE'S LADY BUG

Tail:	Red squirrel tail	Shellback:	Fluorescent pink chenille
Body:	Brown chenille	Rib:	Oval gold tinsel, binding down
Hackle:	Fluorescent orange palmered for-		the shellback
	ward		

Pete's Lady Bug, a wet fly reminiscent of both nymph and shrimp type flies, is well-known as a top producer on the Thompson River in British Columbia. It was developed by Pete Peterson of Vancouver, B.C.

Tied by Kelvin McKay

PHEASANT SPEY

Tag:	Flat silver tinsel		loop and wrapped over the seal
Body:	Rear ⅔: Flat silver tinsel		only
	Front ⅓: Claret seal fur or substi-	Throat:	Several turns of golden pheasant
	tute		rump
Rib:	Silver wire	Wing:	Two golden pheasant breast feath-
Body hackle: Gray-green ringneck rump			ers tied flat on top of one another
	feather, twisted onto a dubbing		

This is a very simple, killing Spey dressed by Cliff Barker of Bellevue, Washington, who fishes it on a sink-tip line from early spring into the late fall. Barker is well known among steelheaders in the Northwest for his skill as a fisherman and his long-time use of a two-hand Spey rod. This example is tied on a gold-plated "Alec Jackson Spey Hook."

Tied by Cliff Barker

Tied by Mike Mercer

PINK SALMON

Tail:	Fluorescent pink marabou and pink crystal flash	Collar:	Fluorescent orange hackle
Body:	Fuchsia crystal chenille	Head:	Silver bead chain eyes and fluorescent red thread
Hackle:	Fluorescent pink palmered forward		

This fly was originated in 1988 by Mike Mercer of the Fly Shop in Redding, California, for Alaskan king and silver salmon. The Pink Salmon has also been an extremely productive steelhead pattern in both Alaska and British Columbia, and most notably on the the Dean River in August and September.

Tied by Umpqua Feather Merchants

POLAR SHRIMP

Tail:	Red hackle barbs	Collar:	Orange hackle
Body:	Orange or fluorescent orange chenille	Wing:	Natural polar bear or white bucktail

The Polar Shrimp dates back to the mid 1930s when it was extremely popular in Northern California on the Eel River. It is unclear who invented the pattern, but there is little doubt about the effectiveness of this bright fly for steelhead. The early examples were produced prior to the availability of fluorescent chenille; today it is most often tied using this brighter material. It should not be confused with another pattern of the same name that was tied by Martin Tolley.

Tied by John Olschewsky

POLAR SHRIMP, GLASSO

Tip:	Silver twist		twist along the back edge of the tinsel
Tail:	Red hackle barbs		
Body:	Rear ½: Fluorescent orange floss	Hackle:	Red, palmered over the seal fur
	Front ½: Fluorescent orange seal fur	Throat:	Dark pink
		Wing:	Strips of white goose wing quill
Rib:	Flat silver tinsel followed by silver	Head:	Red

This is a variation of the original Polar Shrimp tied in the style of the late Syd Glasso by John Olschewsky of Enumclaw, Washington. John uses this fly throughout the winter. For use in fast water he substitutes a hair wing; in slow pools he uses soft marabou.

Tied by Mark Waslick

POLAR SHRIMP, HAAS

Tag:	Flat gold tinsel	Collar:	Orange hackle
Body:	Orange seal fur	Wing:	White arctic fox, polar bear, or calftail
Rib:	Oval gold tinsel		

This Polar Shrimp was tied by Mark Waslick using the reverse-wing technique developed by the late Ed Haas of Forks of the Salmon, California. Haas, a professional fly dresser, produced his virtually indestructible hairwing flies by opening the return eye loop of a salmon hook and securing the hair into the opening with the tips facing forward. After the tail, body and hackles were tied the tying thread was brought ahead of the wing which was then folded back and secured with wraps of thread in the front.

POOR MAN'S G.P.

Body:	Flat gold tinsel			marabou
Collar:	About half a dozen turns of folded stiff fluorescent orange hackle, in front of which are an equal number of turns of fluorescent orange	Wing:	Two red golden pheasant body feathers tied flat on top
		Front collar:	1½ turns of bronze mallard
		Head:	Red

This simple marabou-shrimp pattern was designed in 1980 by Russ Miller of Arlington, Washington. Miller has been quite successful in his effort to create an effective substitute for the difficult-to-tie General Practitioner.

Tied by Russ Miller

POPSICLE

Wing (1):	Tied about ⅔ of the way up the hook shank: Orange marabou around which is gold and purple Flashabou	Wing (2):	Cherry-red fluorescent marabou
		Collar:	Purple schlappen hackle
		Head:	Fluorescent red

George Cook originated the Popsicle as a silver-salmon fly while he was guiding in Alaska in the early 1980s. It has proven to be his most popular pattern for winter steelhead from northern Oregon up into British Columbia on rivers like the Dean, Babine and Kispiox. Cook varies the quantity of Flashabou in each fly to suit his needs: heavy amounts for salmon or steelhead in high water, and lesser amounts for low water, or shy steelhead. See also Showgirl.

Tied by George Cook

PRICHARD'S WESTERN ANGLER

Tail:	Red calftail	Throat:	Purple hackle barbs
Body:	Black chenille	Wing:	White polar bear or substitute with a shorter topping of orange calftail
Rib:	Oval gold tinsel		

This is a variation of the Skunk originated in the early 1980s by Wayne Orzel, proprietor of Prichard's Western Anglers on the Kalama River in Washington. Orzel, who spends much of his free time fishing, feels that the subtle color changes make this pattern even better on the Kalama River than the standard Skunk.

Tied by Wayne Orzel

PURPLE BAD HABIT

Tail:	Purple marabou, full		as the wing
Body:	Silver braided Mylar tinsel	Hackle:	A turn or two of red, purple, and magenta wound through each other
Wing:	Purple over which is magenta Flashabou		
Throat:	Purple marabou the same length	Head:	Fluorescent orange

The Purple Bad Habit was designed for silver salmon by Don Hathaway while guiding out of Bristol Bay Lodge in Alaska. Over time it has proved to be even better for steelhead throughout the rivers in the northwest.

Tied by Mark Waslick

Tied by John Shewey

PURPLE BRAT

Tag:	Flat gold tinsel and fluorescent orange floss	Collar:	Purple hackle
		Wing:	White over which is purple polar bear or substitute
Tail:	Golden pheasant crest dyed orange	Cheeks:	Jungle cock
Body:	Rear two-fifths: Orange seal fur Front three-fifths: Purple seal fur	Note:	An optional collar of guinea fowl or teal flank dyed purple may be added after the wing is applied
Rib:	Oval gold tinsel		

The Purple Brat is a variation of Enos Bradner's 1937 classic Stillaguamish favorite, Brad's Brat. The Purple Brat was invented by Dave McNeese, of Salem, Oregon, and has proven very effective on the rivers of northern and central Oregon.

Tied by John Shewey

PURPLE FLAME HILTON

Tag:	Flat silver tinsel and fluorescent red floss	Rib:	Oval silver tinsel
		Wing:	A pair of grizzly hackle tips curving away from one another
Tail:	Fluorescent red floss	Collar:	Guinea fowl dyed purple
Body:	Rear ⅓: Red-orange seal fur Front ⅔: Purple seal fur	Head:	Claret

This variation of the Silver Hilton, originated in the 1970s by Dave McNeese of McNeese's Fly Fishing Shop in Salem, Oregon, is notable on the Willamette River system at mid-day during periods of low-water.

Tied by Joe Howell

PURPLE PERIL

Tag:	Embossed silver tinsel (optional)	Wing:	Brown bucktail or red squirrel tail
Tail:	Purple hackle barbs	Note:	May also be dressed dry with the following changes: Body: Purple floss; Rib: Flat silver tinsel
Body:	Purple chenille		
Rib:	Oval or embossed silver tinsel		
Collar:	Soft purple hackle		

The Purple Peril was originated in the late 1930s or early 1940s. It is credited to Ken McLeod who, as the story goes, asked his son George to order dyed-claret materials from Herter's catalog to tie some Montreals. What Herter's sent was clearly purple, not claret. McLeod tied the fly anyway and the Purple Peril was born. It is commonly fished wet and is effective in clear to slightly off-colored water.

Tied by Al Buhr

PURPLE RED-BUTT

Tag:	Flat silver tinsel	Rib:	Oval silver tinsel
Butt:	Fluorescent red floss or poly yarn	Collar:	Purple hackle
Tail:	Bright red hackle barbs	Wing:	Two purple hen hackles set high and splayed out
Body:	Purple seal fur or substitute		

This pattern came from Keith Burkhardt's Valley Flyfisher shop, in Salem, Oregon. It was originated by Al Buhr from Keizer, Oregon, who ties flies for the Valley Flyfisher and is well known for his innovative style of dressing steelhead flies. This fly has been very effective locally on the North Santiam as well as on the Deschutes River.

PURPLE SKUNK

Tail:	Gray squirrel tail	Rib:	Oval silver tinsel
Butt:	Fluorescent green chenille	Collar:	Purple hackle
Body:	Purple chenille	Wing:	Gray squirrel tail

The Purple Skunk is one of the better known patterns to have originated on Idaho's Clearwater River. It is the product of Keith Stonebreaker of Lewiston, Idaho, who combined elements borrowed from the Skunk and the Purple Peril.

Tied by Dick Stewart

PURPLE SUNRISE

Tail:	Mixed orange and red hackle barbs	Collar:	Long, soft orange hackle
Body:	Purple Poly Flash	Wing:	Purple calftail or bucktail
Hackle:	Red palmered forward	Head:	Light blue Poly Flash

Dave Hall originated the Purple Sunrise in 1982 on a rainy evening at camp on the Babine River in British Columbia. Concerned about the fact that the rain would discolor the water and raise the level of the river, Dave sat down after supper and tried to work up a few bright patterns that would be visible to the steelhead the next day. The Purple Sunrise took the only fish caught the next day and has continued to produce on every river where it's been fished.

Tied by Dave Hall

PURPLE UGLY

Tail:	Claret calftail	Collar:	Fluorescent red hackle
Body:	Purple yarn	Wing:	Claret calftail
Rib:	Flat silver tinsel	Head:	Bead chain eyes and red thread

The Purple Ugly is one of several fly patterns originated by British Columbia steelhead guide Gary Miltenberger of Steelhead Valhalla Lodge. Originally tied for the Bella Coola River winter run, it has proven equally effective on the Kispiox and Babine as well as for summer-run fish on the Dean.

Tied by Farrow Allen

QUARTER POUNDER

Body:	Fluorescent green, yellow, orange, pink or red chenille		tied in at the head and unbraided
Wing:	Pearlescent braided Mylar tubing,	Head:	Fluorescent thread that complements the body color

Vermonters Jim Christman, a guide and charter boat captain, and Mark Quinlan developed this successful pattern for New York's Salmon River in 1982. They called it the Quarter Pounder because ". . . it looked exactly like a new shiny quarter rolling across the gravel bottom." It is a very effective fly tied in all of the color combinations suggested.

Tied by Tom Clark

QUILCEDA

Tied by Karen Gobin

Tag:	A single turn of flat silver tinsel	Rib:	Flat silver tinsel
Body:	Rear ¼: Gray seal fur or substitute	Hackle:	Pheasant rump feather dyed dark red
	Forward ¾: Fiery brown seal fur or substitute	Head:	Claret

This fly was originated by Karen Gobin about 1985. It is a pattern that has been particularly effective for summer fishing on the North Fork of the Stillaguamish. Gobin named it after the Quilceda, a small creek that runs past her house in Marysville before emptying into Puget Sound, north of Seattle.

RED ANT

Tied by Scott Ripley

Tag:	Flat silver tinsel	Body:	Red floss
Tail:	Golden pheasant tippet or red hackle barbs	Collar:	Brown hackle
		Wing:	Natural brown bucktail
Butt:	Peacock herl	Cheeks:	Jungle cock (optional)

The Red Ant is considered an indispensable fly on Oregon's Rogue River. Its origin as a trout fly dates back to the days of Izaak Walton and a nearly identical pattern by the same name. As a steelhead pattern it has been around since Mike Kennedy introduced this dressing in the 1940s.

RED SHRIMP

Tied by Walt Johnson

Tag:	One turn of flat silver tinsel		second turn of tinsel
Body:	Red fur loosely dubbed over fluorescent orange floss	Collar:	Soft red hackle, tied back
Rib:	Flat silver tinsel	Wing:	Hen hackle tips or strips of wing quill, dyed red-claret, short and low
Body hackle: Dark ringneck pheasant rump feather palmered forward from the		Topping:	Golden pheasant crest
		Head:	Red

The Red Shrimp was tied in the 1950s by Walt Johnson after a trip with Ralph Wahl to the Upper Columbia River. During a streamside encounter, a local angler showed them his favorite fly: a crude red-orange pattern that was deadly on the stretch of water where the Entiat and Methow entered the Columbia. The meeting produced a lasting friendship and provided the inspiration for the Red Shrimp.

REDWING

Tied by John Shewey

Tag:	Flat silver tinsel		the head of the fly
Tail:	Golden pheasant crest	Wing:	Jungle cock eyes, back to back, covered by a pair of matched golden pheasant tippets
Body:	Rear ½: Light orange floss, ribbed with fine silver wire		
	Front ½: Red macaw or white hen breast feathers dyed red, tied in bunches along the sides of the hook shank, tapering up towards	Cheeks:	Jungle cock veiled by a pair of hen breast feathers dyed red
		Topping:	Golden pheasant crest
		Head:	Red

This is John Shewey's dressing of an attractive pattern that was originated in 1982 by Dave McNeese of Salem, Oregon. In Trey Combs' *Steelhead Fly Fishing* the fly is described as being used "in quiet pools and tailouts."

REDWING BLACKBIRD

Tail: Red hackle barbs
Body: Two layers of fine black chenille
Rib: Silver wire
Throat: Guinea fowl hackle dyed red

Wing: Red calftail
Head: Black thread built up to correspond with the size of the body

The Redwing Blackbird was originated by Ray Baker of Eugene, Oregon, as a variation of the Skunk. Since its introduction in 1985, it has grown steadily in popularity throughout southern Oregon and northern California.

Tied by Kent Bulfinch

RED/BLUE SPEY

Tag: Flat silver tinsel
Body: Red seal fur or substitute
Rib: Oval silver tinsel
Hackle: Long guinea fowl dyed teal blue and palmered Spey style from

about the second turn of tinsel
Collar: Guinea fowl dyed red, shorter than the body hackle
Head: Red

A basic Spey-type fly designed by Bob Borden of Monroe, Oregon, it's tied with easily procured guinea fowl. Borden is the originator of several popular patterns including the Krystal Bullet. He is also the owner of Hareline Products, a manufacturer and distributor of fly-tying materials.

Tied by Bob Borden

RENEGADE

Tag: Gold tinsel
Rear hackle: Brown
Body: Peacock herl (may be ribbed with

fine wire for reinforcement)
Front hackle: White

The Renegade is best known as one of the West's outstanding trout flies that is widely fished both wet and dry. As a steelhead pattern it is fished wet, and is one of the most productive flies on Oregon's Rogue River. It is often tied on a double hook to give the fly additional weight.

Tied by Kent Bulfinch

RICHEY'S GOLDEN GIRL

Tail: Golden-orange calftail
Body: Gold tinsel chenille
Throat: Golden-orange calftail

Wing: Golden-orange calftail
Head: Red

Originated in 1969 by Chuck Lunn of Flint, Michigan, and George Richey as "an attractor pattern with lots of flash," the Golden Girl is usually tied in smaller sizes (8 or 10) and is fished in both the spring and fall.

Tied by George Richey

Tied by George Richey

RICHEY'S PLATTE RIVER PINK

Tail:	Pale pink Glo-Bug yarn or imitation hair		tion hair
		Wing:	White calftail
Body:	Fluorescent pink chenille	Head:	Red
Throat:	Pale pink Glo-Bug yarn or imita-		

This bright attractor pattern was introduced by George Richey in 1973. It has performed well on Michigan steelhead rivers under varying conditions, notably on the clear water of the Platte River as well as on the more discolored Betsie River.

Tied by John Shewey

RICK'S REVENGE

Tag:	Flat silver tinsel	Wing:	White over which is purple polar bear or substitute
Tail:	A strand of fluorescent pink floss		
Body:	Rear ½: Fluorescent pink floss veiled over the top with a strand of the same floss	Collar (2):	Guinea fowl dyed deep purple and slightly longer than the first collar
	Front ½: Deep purple dubbing	Cheek:	Jungle cock, ½ body length
Rib:	Fine oval silver tinsel over the purple dubbing	Head:	Red
		Note:	A variation substitutes fluorescent red floss for the pink
Collar (1): Purple hackle			

Designed in 1986 through a joint effort between guide Rick Wren and John Shewey, this fly has been successful on the Deschutes River.

Tied by Farrow Allen

ROGUE RIVER SPECIAL

Hook:	Most often tied on a a small double hook for fishing the Rogue River	Rib:	Flat silver tinsel
		Collar:	Brown
Tail:	Mixed red and white bucktail	Wing:	Mixed red and white bucktail, tied upright and divided
Butt:	Yellow wool		
Body:	Red wool		

The divided, upright wing on this wet fly is the development of years of collective experience on Oregon's Rogue River. Successful guides on the lower sections of the Rogue feel that this fly, of which there are many variations, should be cast almost directly downstream (usually from a drift boat), permitted to hang in the current and twitched slightly.

Tied by Steve Gobin

ROSE PETAL

Tag:	Flat silver tinsel and fluorescent pink floss over flat silver tinsel, ribbed with very fine flat silver tinsel	Body:	Light claret seal fur or substitute
		Rib:	Flat silver tinsel
		Hackle:	Pheasant rump feather dyed light claret and palmered over body
Tail:	Golden pheasant tippets dyed claret	Wing:	White skunk hair
		Collar:	Guinea fowl hackle

Originated by Steve Gobin of Marysville, Washington. Gobin, a member of the Tulalip Tribe, fishes commercially for salmon and works in forestry management. He is a skilled fly tier and in his spare time he fishes for steelhead and cutthroat trout. Steve is recognized as one of Washington's skilled tiers of classic Atlantic-salmon flies.

ROYAL COACHMAN BUCKTAIL

Tail:	Golden pheasant tippets	Collar:	Brown hackle
Body:	⅛ peacock herl, ⅜ scarlet floss, ½ peacock herl	Wing:	White hair

Unquestionably, in one form or another, the Royal Coachman has been one of the most popular and successful patterns for more than a century. Its only fault is the fragile nature of the peacock herl which may come undone even before a steelhead takes a bite of it. This can be avoided by adding a rib of fine gold wire and/or coating the hook shank with cement before wrapping the peacock herl.

Tied by Dick Stewart

R.V.I.

Tag:	Flat silver tinsel	Rib:	Oval silver tinsel
Tail:	Golden pheasant body feather barbs	Hackle:	Teal over the front ⅔, optionally counter-wrapped with fine gold wire
Body:	Rear ⅓: Pearl Flashabou or flat silver tinsel	Wing:	Four red golden pheasant body feathers, set low over the body
	Front ⅔: Orange seal fur or substitute	Head:	Fluorescent red

R.V.I. represents the initials of the originator, Ronald Van Iderstine, a steelhead guide from Springfield, Oregon. The R.V.I. may also be dressed with a forebody of purple, green, or light-orange fur. Trey Combs in his book *Steelhead Fly Fishing* tells that this fly is reputed to having risen ". . . 10 fish and landed seven on my best evening with the light-orange version."

Tied by Mark Waslick

SALMON RIVER CARDINELLE

Body:	Fluorescent green chenille		fluorescent green marabou
Collar:	Pearlescent Mylar tubing	Head:	Fluorescent green or yellow
Wing:	Fluorescent green hair over which		

Beginning in the early 1980s, an increasing number of northeastern anglers were fishing to the impressive runs of steelhead and salmon that entered New York's Salmon River, South Sandy Creek and Grindstone Creek, all tributaries of Lake Ontario. Fluorescent green was rapidly proving to be one of the most effective colors for steelhead. The Salmon River Cardinelle, a variation of Paul Kukonen's cerise Cardinelle streamer, was introduced by Farrow Allen in 1981 as a steelhead fly on the Salmon River.

Tied by Farrow Allen

SANTIAM SPECTRUM SPEY

Tag:	Flat silver tinsel	Hackle:	Purple Spey hackle over the seal fur
Body:	Rear ½: Fluorescent red floss		
	Front ½: Deep purple seal fur or substitute	Wing:	Strands of fluorescent pink, orange and red silk floss, over which is bronze mallard
Rib:	Oval gold tinsel, counter wrapped with oval gold wire	Head:	Pale gray

This Spey type fly was designed for use on Oregon's North Santiam by John Shewey who says ". . . when viewed under water from behind and below - the way a steelhead sees a fly - the colored strands of floss show sufficiently to flash a bit of color . . . while the bronze mallard holds everything in place."

Tied by John Shewey

Wet Flies

Tied by Farrow Allen

Tied by Ray Schmidt

Tied by Frank Lendzion

Tied by George Cook

SARP'S SEDUCER

Tail:	Pearl Flashabou, tied full and about one-third the length of the hook		each color
Body:	Gold or pearlescent braided Mylar tubing over optional lead wire	Topping:	Medium blue Flashabou completely covering the marabou
Wing:	Red marabou over which is black marabou, tied full, two plumes of	Eyes:	Silver bead chain or lead eyes
		Head:	Red

Sarp's Seducer is a non-traditional but very effective fly pattern from Tony Sarp of Everett, Washington, owner and operator of Katmai Lodge in Alaska. The Seducer has been exceptionally effective in British Columbia where it is usually tied on large hooks, up to size 5/0, and fished deep.

SCHMIDT'S WOOLLY SPEY

Tag:	Fluorescent red (or green) yarn		several additional turns taken at the head to form a collar
Body:	Mottled brown wool		
Hackle:	Brown schlappen hackle tied in by the tip and palmered forward with	Note:	May be weighted with wraps of lead wire

Schmidt's Woolly Spey was introduced to Michigan steelhead rivers in 1987 by Ray Schmidt of Wellston, Michigan. It has proved very effective on the Manistee from late spring through midsummer, fished quartering downstream on a sink-tip line. An excellent variation is tied with a a body of black crystal chenille and palmered with black schlappen hackle.

SCREAMING WOODSIE

Body:	Pearl Kreinick Tyer's Ribbon, pearl Poly Flash or pearlescent braided Mylar tubing	Topping:	About four strands each of peacock herl and multi-color crystal flash
Throat:	White calf body hair	Cheeks:	Jungle cock body feather
Wing:	Two pair of grizzly hackles		

The Screaming Woodsie was sent to us by Frank Lendzion of the Wellston Inn in Wellston, Michigan. He describes it as a good pattern for taking fish that are holding in tight cover such as log jams and undercut banks. "It was first fished by Bob Wood in the late 1970s when he hooked six steelhead over 14 pounds... and the only sounds were the screams of Bob Wood."

SHOWGIRL

Body:	None		topping of purple Flashabou
Wing:	Cerise marabou, mostly on top but some of which ends up under the hook shank. Over this is a	Collar:	Purple schlappen hackle or marabou
		Head:	Fluorescent red

The Showgirl was the first and one of the most successful of the so-called Alaskabou patterns developed by George Cook when he was guiding in Alaska at the Alagnak Lodge. After running out of appropriate saddle hackle Cook substituted marabou, resulting in a new series of marabou winter flies that includes the Tequila Sunrise, Popsicle, Candy Cane and Pixie's Revenge.

SIGNAL LIGHT

Tail:	Dark purple hackle barbs	Rib:	Fine oval silver tinsel
Body:	First ¼: Fluorescent red-orange yarn	Wing:	Very sparse strands of blue, pearl, lime, and wine crystal flash over which is black marabou
	Second ¼: Fluorescent green yarn		
	Front ½: Black chenille	Collar:	Soft, dark purple hackle

This pattern was designed by Randall Kaufmann of Kaufmann's Streamborn Fly Fishing Shops in Washington and Oregon. He describes it as a personal favorite and one of the best-selling patterns in his shops. It's named after the combination of colors in the fly which are reminiscent of the signal lights along the railroad tracks that border the Deschutes River.

Tied by Randall Kaufmann

SILVER ANT

Hook:	Traditionally tied on a small double	Wing:	White bucktail, often tied upright and divided
Tail:	Red hackle barbs	Cheeks:	Jungle cock
Butt:	Black chenille	Collar:	Black hackle
Body:	Oval silver tinsel		

The high-winged Silver Ant is a typical Rogue River fly that was originated in the 1930s by either I.R. Towers of Coos Bay, Oregon, or by Mike Kennedy of Lake Oswego, Oregon. Regardless, it quickly became a standard pattern that remains popular today.

Tied by Farrow Allen

SILVER DOCTOR

Body:	Flat silver tinsel		calftail over which is barred teal flank
Throat:	Turquoise blue hackle barbs		
Wing:	Yellow calftail over which is red	Head:	Red

Bill McMillan tied this variation of the classic Atlantic salmon fly in 1971 during a period of experimentation while attempting to "follow the greased-line method in its application to steelhead." Over the years this pattern has proven effective in the fall and particularly in tannin-stained water.

Tied by Bill McMillan

SILVER HILTON

Tail:	Mallard flank or red hackle barbs	Wing:	A pair of grizzly hackle tips curving away from one another
Body:	Black chenille		
Rib:	Flat or oval silver tinsel	Collar:	Soft grizzly hackle

A good drab-colored fly on most west coast rivers, the Silver Hilton originated around 1950 on the Klamath and Trinity rivers of northern California, where it is still tremendously popular. Although it bears some resemblance to the Skunk, the delicate hackle-tip wings of the Silver Hilton "breathe" in a tantalizing fashion when caught in the river currents.

Tied by Umpqua Feather Merchants

SILVER HILTON, GREEN BUTT

Tag:	Silver tinsel	Rib:	Oval silver tinsel
Tail:	Pintail flank barbs	Wing:	Paired grizzly hackles, curving away from one another
Butt:	Fluorescent green seal fur or substitute		
Body:	Black seal fur or substitute	Collar:	Teal, pintail or gadwall flank feather

Originated by Dave McNeese, this variation of the Silver Hilton has much in common with the Green Butt Skunk. Often, the addition of a hot spot of fluorescent color on the butt of a dark fly makes the difference that can excite a stubborn fish into action. The Irish Hilton is yet another variation that replaces the tail with peacock-sword barbs.

Tied by John Shewey

SILVER HILTON, PEACOCK

Tail:	Teal flank barbs	Wing:	Broad grizzly hackle tips, curving away from one another
Body:	Peacock herl		
Rib:	Oval silver tinsel	Collar:	Grizzly hackle

This popular variation of the well-known Silver Hilton was designed by André Puyans of Creative Sports Enterprises in Pleasant Hills, California. The Peacock Hilton, as it is also known, was developed in the late 1960s and is often fished with good results on a dead drift as well as with a conventional swing.

Tied by André Puyans

SIMMY SPECIAL

Body:	Green chenille	Wing:	Mallard flank tied flat on top
Hackle:	Brown, palmered over the body		

This is an old fly from Simmy Nolf who, from the 1940s through the 1960s, guided for steelhead on the Pere Marquette and other Michigan rivers. Nolf has devoted much of his life to fishing and working to preserve a quality steelhead fishery in Michigan, and he has been called "the oldest living river keeper." He originated the Simmy Special in the 1940s and a half century later his original dressing is still effective.

Tied by Simmy Nolf

SKAGIT SPECIAL

Body:	Flat silver tinsel		ange marabou, each tied in by the tip and wound forward in front of the shoulder
Shoulder:	Orange seal fur or substitute, dubbed over the forward part of the body		
Hackle:	Yellow marabou followed by or-	Collar:	Teal or guinea fowl
		Head:	Red

A variation of Aid's Red and Orange Marabou, this fly dates from the early 1980s. Aid's Black and Orange, Pink and Red and the Pinky (blue and pink) have all proven to be excellent winter and early-spring patterns in Washington state. They are also effective whenever the water is high, even in summer.

Tied by Bob Aid

SKUNK

Tail:	Red hackle barbs	Collar:	Black hackle
Body:	Black chenille or wool	Wing:	White skunk hair or substitute
Rib:	Flat or oval silver tinsel		

Some believe that the first Skunk was tied for the Stillaguamish River during the 1930s by Wes Drain of Seattle, Washington. Joe Howell of Idleyld Park, Oregon, believes the Skunk originated on the North Umpqua River during the early 1940s. Regardless, the Skunk is one of the most popular steelhead fly patterns in use.

Tied by Bill Logan

SKUNK, GREEN BUTT

Tail:	Red hackle barbs	Collar:	Soft black hackle
Butt:	Fluorescent green chenille or yarn	Wing:	White hair (polar bear, bucktail, calftail, or, if you dare, white skunk hair)
Body:	Black chenille		
Rib:	Flat or oval silver tinsel		

This is a popular variation of the Skunk - possibly the most widely used steelhead pattern of all. The idea of adding a fluorescent-green butt to a standard dressing may have come from Atlantic-salmon fishermen who have enjoyed great success with fluorescent-butt flies.

Tied by Umpqua Feather Merchants

SKUNK, GREEN BUTT SPEY

Tag:	Flat silver tinsel and fluorescent green floss ribbed with flat silver tinsel, over a flat silver tinsel underbody	Rib:	Oval silver tinsel
		Hackle:	Black schlappen hackle palmered over the black dubbing
		Wing:	White skunk hair
Tail:	Red hackle barbs	Collar:	Speckled guinea hackle
Body:	Black Sealex (seal fur substitute)		

This variation of the well-known Green Butt Skunk was designed and dressed by Steve Gobin of Marysville, Washington. It is meticulously tied in Steve's classically-oriented style and typifies what you would find in one of his working boxes of flies.

Tied by Steve Gobin

SKUNK, RED BUTT

Tail:	Red hackle barbs	Rib:	Flat or oval silver tinsel
Butt:	Red chenille or yarn	Collar:	Soft black hackle
Body:	Black chenille or yarn	Wing:	White calftail

There isn't much difference between this and the Green Butt Skunk, but on some occasions, even the slightest change in a fly pattern can make a difference to the fish. The addition of a colored butt to the Skunk substantially increases its effectiveness in a range of situations; in some instances the red butt provides a good change of pace.

Tied by Umpqua Feather Merchants

Tied by Michael Malloy

SKYKOMISH PURPLE

Body:	Rear ½: Purple floss	Throat:	Guinea fowl dyed purple
	Front ½: Purple dubbing	Wing:	Two narrow red golden pheasant
Rib:	Oval gold tinsel		body feathers, set low and flat over
Hackle:	Ringneck pheasant rump feather,		the body
	dyed purple, palmered over the	Head:	Claret
	front half of the body		

This attractive purple fly was originated during the late 1980s by Michael Malloy of Everett, Washington. It is an effective pattern for both summer- and winter-run fish on most rivers in northern Washington, including the Skykomish and the North Fork of the Stillaguamish.

Tied by Russ Miller

SKYKOMISH SUNRISE

Tag:	Silver tinsel (optional)	Collar:	Red and yellow hackle wound to-
Tail:	Mixed red and yellow hackle barbs,		gether
	or red on top of yellow	Wing:	White calftail or bucktail
Body:	Red chenille	Head:	Red or black
Rib:	Flat or oval silver tinsel		

The Skykomish Sunrise is a standard on nearly every river where steelhead are fished. It was introduced in 1940 by the father-and-son angling partnership of Ken and George McLeod. As the story is told by Bob Arnold, a skilled fly tier and angler in his own right, Ken asked his son George to "tie me a fly the color of the sky."

Tied by Fran Verdoliva

SMOLT

Tail:	Rainbow Lure Flash (multicolored		Front ⅓: Red Estaz chenille
	strands of Mylar)	Shellback:	Same as tail
Body:	Rear ⅔: White Estaz chenille	Head:	Fluorescent green

This fly was originated by Fran Verdoliva as an impressionistic imitation of rainbow-trout smolt. During the spring it is fished quartering downstream in and around occupied spawning beds where it frequently aggravates steelhead into striking. Verdoliva, a full-time steelhead guide on the Salmon River in New York, says that for the last three seasons the Smolt has been his most effective spring pattern.

Tied by Bob Veverka

SOL DUC SPEY

Body:	Rear ½: Fluorescent orange floss		one side stripped, palmered for-
	Front ½: Fluorescent orange seal		ward from the second turn of tin-
	fur or substitute		sel
Rib:	Flat silver tinsel	Throat:	Black heron substitute
Hackle:	Long webby yellow hackle with	Wing:	Four fluorescent orange hackles

The Sol Duc, Sol Duc Spey and Sol Duc Dark are are three elegant flies that were introduced by Syd Glasso and are successfully fished on the Sol Duc and other wild rivers of the dark and shadowy Olympic rain forest. The largest fly-caught steelhead in the United States in 1959 weighed almost 19 pounds and was caught by Glasso in the winter on a Sol Duc fly in the Sol Duc River.

SPADE

Tail: Fine natural deer hair   Hackle: Grizzly
Body: Black chenille

Bob Arnold of Seattle, Washington, originated the Spade in the early 1960s for the North Fork of the Stillaguamish River. During that particular season the water on the North Fork had been low all summer and the brighter, fuller patterns seemed to spook the fish. Arnold designed this simple, drab, more buoyant, wingless fly to pass through a pool without hanging up on the bottom or otherwise scaring the steelhead. About the same time, Bob Wintle of British Columbia designed a nearly identical pattern for the Morice and Bulkley Rivers that he called Wintle's Western Wizard.

Tied by Bob Arnold

SPADE, CLARET GUINEA

Butt: Fluorescent red yarn or ostrich herl dyed red
Tail: Fine deer body hair, dark brown mink or fitch tail
Body: Black chenille or black ostrich herl
       twisted with fine oval silver tinsel
Collar: Grizzly cock hackle followed by a longer, claret dyed guinea fowl

This variation of the original Spade (see above) was developed by Alec Jackson of Kenmore, Washington, in the early 1980s. Jackson is the designer of the Alec Jackson Spey Hook shown here, and is also an active steelhead conservationist. The Claret Guinea Spade is an effective fall pattern that is normally fished on a slow-sinking ten-foot sink-tip line, either in the early morning or the failing light of dusk.

Tied by Alec Jackson

SPADE, INLAND

Hook: Fine wire dry fly
Tail: Fine natural deer body hair
Body: Black ostrich herl twisted with fine
       oval silver tinsel for reinforcement
Collar: Soft grizzly hackle
Head: Fluorescent red

As steelhead make their way up the Columbia River and enter the tributaries where they eventually spawn, they undergo changes, possibly including the partial loss of vision. With this in mind, Alec Jackson designed the Inland Spade in the late 1970s for late-season fishing east of the Cascades. The heavy dressing provides a strong silhouette and keeps the fly in an ideal position - within an inch to an inch and a half of the surface.

Tied by Alec Jackson

SPADE, WHAKA BLOND

Tail: Purple hackle barbs
Body: Purple ostrich twisted with fine oval silver tinsel for reinforcement
Collar: Soft purple hackle
Head: Fluorescent red

Alec Jackson of Kenmore, Washington, provides us with this all-purple Spade variation. The Whaka Blond was developed in the early 1980s and was named for Whakarewrewa, a district on New Zealand's Central North Island where there is some fairly good fly fishing for transplanted coastal steelhead. It is a productive alternate pattern for the Wenatchee and Skykomish Rivers.

Tied by Alec Jackson

Tied by John Shewey

Tied by Walt Johnson

Tied by Dick Stewart

Tied by Walt Johnson

SPAWNING PURPLE SPEY

Tag:	Flat silver tinsel, long	Collar:	Deep purple hackle in front of which is barred teal of equal length
Tail:	Purple hackle barbs (sometimes omitted)	Wing:	A pair of peacock or mottled turkey secondary wing quill segments enveloping the upper edge of the hackle
Body:	Fluorescent red floss over flat silver tinsel		
Underwing:	Five spikes of purple marabou, tied in at equal intervals on the front half of the body	Cheeks:	Jungle cock (optional)
		Head:	Claret

This strikingly beautiful fly was developed in 1986 by writer and angler John Shewey of Aumsville, Oregon, for winter-run fish. The purple marabou "spikes" of this sparse-bodied fly provide a lot of movement for grease-line fishing.

SPECTRAL SPIDER

Tail:	Fluorescent yellow Antron or craft fur fibers		green and blue Antron flanked on either side by a shorter light badger hackle tip
Body:	Flat silver tinsel or pearlescent Mylar	Collar:	Mallard breast tied spider style
Wing:	Sparse bunches of cerise, orange,	Cheek:	Blue kingfisher substitute

Walt Johnson of Arlington, Washington, began tying this fly in the 1970s for coastal cutthroat trout entering the North Fork of the Stillaguamish. It soon became evident that the Spectral Spider fished either wet, dry, or in the surface film also was very effective on steelhead and silver salmon. To tie this pattern as a dry-fly, substitute golden-pheasant-crest fibers for the tail, take several turns of stiff grizzly hackle before winding the mallard, and make the wing sparse.

SPEY DAY

Tag:	Oval gold tinsel	Hackle:	Gray heron substitute palmered forward over the entire body along the rib
Body:	In three equal sections: Light orange, dark orange, and scarlet dubbing		
		Wing:	Dyed light orange bucktail
Rib:	Oval gold tinsel	Cheek:	Black and white barred woodduck

Scott Byner developed this Spey pattern for early summer-run steelhead in Alaska. It has been used successfully on most of the steelhead rivers of Prince of Wales Island including the Karta, the Klawock and the Harris.

SPRINGER GREEN

Tag:	Flat silver tinsel and fluorescent green floss	Collar:	Soft hackle dyed orange toucan
		Throat:	Barred woodduck
Tail:	Hackle barbs dyed orange toucan	Wing:	Light tan to white rabbit or fox hair
Body:	Rear ½: Light fluorescent yellow-green yarn		
	Front ½: Fluorescent green yarn	Cheeks:	Grass green hackle tips tied high on the wing
Rib:	Flat silver tinsel		

Walt Johnson originated this pattern in the 1970s for fishing to the early run of summer steelhead - known as "Springers" - that enter the lower Columbia River and several of its western tributaries as early as March. These fish are shy but aggressive fighters that respond well to the bright greens and yellows of this fly.

SPRUCE

Tail:	Several peacock sword barbs	Wing:	Pair of badger hackles
Body:	Rear ⅓: Red floss	Collar:	Badger hackle
	Front ⅔: Peacock herl		

Originally the Spruce was tied as a streamer for trout and more specifically for sea-run cutthroat trout. Over time it became clear that migrating summer steelhead were fond of this fly as well. At times the Spruce actually outfishes many of the standard and more traditional patterns. This fly is often tied with the wing secured to the body with oval gold tinsel, Matuka style. If a dark furnace hackle is substituted for the wing and collar the fly is known as a Dark Spruce.

Tied by Dick Stewart

SQUIRREL AND TEAL

Tag:	Oval gold tinsel		a collar)
Tail:	Golden pheasant crest	Wing:	Gray squirrel tail and barred teal
Body:	Gray fur dubbing		flank barbs mixed together and
Rib:	Oval gold tinsel		combed out
Throat:	Blue dun hackle barbs (If jungle	Cheeks:	Jungle cock (optional)
	cock is omitted apply the hackle as		

Harry Lemire originated this pattern in 1969 and usually fishes it on a greased line during the summer. The quiet, neutral tones of this simple gray fly make it very acceptable to wary steelhead lying in shallow runs and slow pools.

Tied by Harry Lemire

STAN OGDEN

Body:	Black wool or poly yarn		tion, palmered forward between
Rib:	Flat silver tinsel		the wraps of tinsel
Hackle:	A badger, furnace or black hackle	Wing:	A single small golden pheasant red
	feather with the barbs clipped short,		rump feather, tied flat
	leaving only the black center por-	Head:	Yellow

This homely little wet fly was devised by Stan Ogden of Vancouver, British Columbia, to catch fish rather than appeal the fisherman's aesthetics. Ogden describes the fly as being ". . . developed for the dour summer-run steelhead on the Morice and Bulkley Rivers . . . when steelhead shy away from large, bright flies but will come to a dark, buggy offering." It has also been fished effectively on the Dean, Thompson, and Coquihalla Rivers.

Tied by Stan Ogden

STEEL WOOLIE, PURPLE

Tail:	Cerise bucktail, twice body length		the tip and palmered forward
Body:	Purple chenille	Collar:	Purple marabou
Hackle:	Purple saddle hackle tied in by	Head:	Red

This effective steelhead fly by Joe Butoric is basically a combination of two popular steelhead fly styles: the Woolly Bugger and the Comet. It may be tied and fished in a variety of color combinations.

Tied by Kaufmann's Streamborn

STEELHEAD BLACK BEAR, DARK

Tied by Joe Rossano

Tag:	Flat gold tinsel	Throat:	A collar of natural black hackle
Tail:	Teal flank	Wing:	Natural black peacock wing quill
Body:	Black bear underfur twisted onto		or turkey wing quill dyed black
	dubbing loop of fine copper wire		

This is one of the best from a series of nine flies by Joe Rossano of Seattle, Washington. Three flies comprise each set and they are tied with bodies of either polar bear, grizzly bear or black bear dubbing, from which they derive their name. Flies of each body fur are then tied with wings of either black, white or oak-brown turkey-wing quill segments, with matching tails. All are tied "semi-low water" style and are intended for clear summer conditions. Rossano says that the style of these flies was inspired by "many years of looking at the color plates in Ray Bergman's *Trout.*"

STEELHEAD SPECTRE

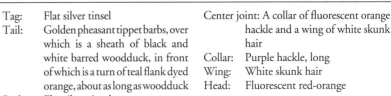

Tied by Bob Veverka

Tag:	Flat silver tinsel	Center joint:	A collar of fluorescent orange
Tail:	Golden pheasant tippet barbs, over		hackle and a wing of white skunk
	which is a sheath of black and		hair
	white barred woodduck, in front	Collar:	Purple hackle, long
	of which is a turn of teal flank dyed	Wing:	White skunk hair
	orange, about as long as woodduck	Head:	Fluorescent red-orange
Body:	Flat silver tinsel		

This original pattern from Bob Veverka of Underhill, Vermont, was designed as a highly-visible pattern for winter fishing in off-colored water.

STEELHEAD SUNSET

Tied by Bob Veverka

Body:	Flat silver tinsel		dyed purple, wound and pulled
Collar:	Yellow, in front of which is or-		down and back
	ange, in front of which is red hackle.	Wing:	Strips of goose wing quills, dyed
	In front of all this is a longer, buff		purple and set low in the Dee style
	ringneck pheasant rump feather	Head:	Fluorescent orange

This winter pattern was also originated by Bob Veverka. Although he lives in Vermont where he is known for his skill in tying streamer flies, he is also known for his superb steelhead and Atlantic-salmon flies. Veverka has committed much time to studying the work of the late Syd Glasso, and his flies reflect this research.

STEWART

Tied by Marty Sherman

Tip:	Flat gold tinsel	Collar:	Soft black hackle
Tail:	Golden pheasant tippet barbs	Wing:	Black calftail over which is a
Body:	Black wool		smaller section of orange calftail
Rib:	Flat gold tinsel		

Marty Sherman, editor of *Flyfishing* magazine, originated this pattern when he was working for Doug Stewart's Fly Shop in Wood Village, Oregon, around 1980. Sherman named the fly after Doug Stewart because the fly was derived from Stewart's popular Max Canyon (which see). Tied sparsely in low-water style, it is a favorite on the Clearwater in Idaho.

STILLAGUAMISH SUNRISE

Tail: Red and yellow hackle barbs
Body: Yellow chenille
Rib: Flat silver tinsel

Collar: Soft orange hackle
Wing: White hair (optional) topped with red crystal flash

An important variation of the Skykomish Sunrise, the Stillaguamish Sunrise tie was designed specifically for Washington's Stillaguamish River, but it has been fished with good results from Idaho to British Columbia. For high-water conditions and winter-run fish, fluorescent chenille and hackle may be substituted.

Tied by Kaufmann's Streamborn

STREET WALKER

Tail: Purple hackle barbs
Body: Purple chenille
Rib: Flat or oval silver tinsel

Collar: Purple hackle
Wing: Clear or pearl Flashabou

Originated in the early 1980s by Gordon Nash, a knowledgeable Deschutes River guide, this is a good summer pattern that the originator likes to dress on a nickel-plated hook.

Tied by Greased Line Fly Shoppe

SUNDOWNER, PURPLE

Tail: Purple hackle barbs
Body: Rear ⅓: Flat silver tinsel
        Front ⅔: Fluorescent orange yarn
Hackle: Purple, palmered over the orange

Wing: yarn
        Pearl crystal flash (originally white calftail)
Collar: Purple hackle

Pink, red, orange, and black are other colors used in this series developed by Bob Wagoner of Lewiston, Idaho. Originated in the mid 1980s, these flies have proven themselves around Lewiston on the Clearwater and Grande Ronde Rivers.

Tied by Farrow Allen

SURGEON GENERAL

Tag: Fine oval silver tinsel (optional)
Tail: Red or fluorescent red hackle barbs
Body: Purple yarn or chenille
Rib: Flat or oval silver tinsel

Throat: Guinea hackle fibers (optional)
Wing: White or fluorescent white bucktail or polar bear or pearl crystal flash
Collar: Red or fluorescent red hackle

There are several variations of this popular pattern combining hair, crystal flash, and plain or fluorescent materials. One story is that the Surgeon General was introduced by an Oregon physician, and named for a well-known neurosurgeon, and became a popular pattern in Washington and Oregon.

Tied by Countrysport

Tied by Teeny Nymph Co.

Tied by Teeny Nymph Co.

Tied by George Cook

Tied by Kelvin McKay

TEENY FLASH FLY

Body: In two equal segments. A bunch of ringneck pheasant tail barbs, dyed black, tied in by the butt ends and wrapped forward to the center of the hook with the balance pulled down to form a beard. The front segment is formed the same way.

Wing: Bleached light ginger pheasant tail barbs over which are about 8 strands of dark crystal flash

This promising new wet-fly variation of the standard Teeny Nymph (which see) was introduced by Jim Teeny in 1990. It is currently being offered by the Teeny Nymph Company with either a black or ginger body and a variety of wing colors.

TEENY LEECH

Tail: Dyed or natural ringneck pheasant tail barbs about the length of the hook shank

Body: A bunch of the same color pheasant barbs wrapped halfway up the hook with the tips pulled down to form a beard at the center of the hook. Repeat the process for the front half of the body.

By modifying his original Teeny Nymph dressing, Jim Teeny has created a leech pattern that is easy to tie and offers more action in the water.

TEQUILA SUNRISE

Rear wing: ⅓ way back on hook shank: Pink marabou, on either side of which are strands of orange crystal flash

Front wing: Salmon-orange marabou on either side of which are strands of orange crystal flash

Collar: Red schlappen hackle

Head: Fluorescent red

This is George Cook's latest addition to his Alaskabou series of flies. Using a popular combination of colors with his method of constructing marabou flies, Cook has produced a fly that has proven deadly on winter-run fish in the Sauk, Skagit and Skykomish Rivers in Washington. When it is tied with crystal flash instead of Flashabou, Cook feels that the Tequila Sunrise is less flashy and more acceptable to steelhead in clear water.

THOMPSON RIVER

Tail: Mixed red and orange or fluorescent orange hackle barbs

Body: Flat copper tinsel

Collar: Mixed red and orange or fluorescent orange hackle, wound together

Wing: Red craft fur over which is a smaller bunch of brown craft fur

This fly was conceived by Walt Johnson in the early 1960s in anticipation of a trip he was making to fish the Thompson River in British Columbia. Johnson's original pattern was tied with bucktail. This craft-hair variation was tied by Kelvin McKay of Cowichan Fly and Tackle in Victoria, British Columbia, where it is more popular than the original.

THOR

Tail:	Orange hackle barbs	Collar:	Soft brown hackle
Body:	Dark red chenille	Wing:	White bucktail

In 1936 C. Jim Pray, a commercial fly tier in Eureka, California, supplied his friend Walter J. Thorsen with his newly designed fly that incorporated the proven colors of the Royal Coachman. On the day this fly was introduced on California's Eel River, Thorsen took his limit of five fish with a combined weight of about sixty pounds, and Pray honored Thorsen by naming the fly Thor.

Tied by Umpqua Feather Merchants

TIGER PAW

Tag:	Oval copper tinsel	Rib:	Oval copper tinsel
Tail:	Black hackle barbs	Wing:	Copper crystal flash
Body:	Black chenille	Collar:	Black hackle

Designed by Joe Howell in the mid 1980s for the Umpqua River summer fish, the Tiger Paw is very effective on the Deschutes and in British Columbia in hook sizes 1 to 1/0, and on the Rogue River in smaller sizes.

Tied by Joe Howell

TOM'S MARABOU MUDDLER

Tail:	Red hackle barbs	strands of peacock herl
Body:	Braided gold Mylar tubing	Head and collar: Natural deer body hair
Wing:	Orange calftail over which is yellow marabou topped with a few	spun and trimmed to shape

Since the mid 1980s Tom Hermant of Yreka, California, has been fishing for steelhead on the Klamath River with this variation of the Marabou Muddler. He declares that it "produces when no other fly seems to be working."

Tied by Tom Hermant

TRANQUILIZER

Tail:	Yellow hackle fibers	Collar:	Purple hackle
Body:	Purple wool or dubbing	Wing:	Finely marked Gray Digger squirrel tail (substitute gray squirrel)
Rib:	Oval gold tinsel, a few turns taken under the tail		

This fly was given to us with high praises by Marty Sherman, the editor of *Flyfishing* magazine. Originally tied by Mike Kennedy in sizes 8 and 10 for the run of Rogue River half-pounders, it was later popularized on the North Umpqua by Ed Hartzel who tied it in larger sizes.

Tied by Marty Sherman

Wet Flies

Tied by Mark Waslick

Tied by Mike Mercer

Tied by Joe Howell

Tied by Bill Logan

TWILIGHT

Tag:	Flat silver tinsel and fluorescent orange floss	Hackle:	Pheasant rump feather dyed black, palmered over the black floss
Tail:	Golden pheasant crest over which is short fluorescent orange floss	Throat:	Guinea fowl dyed blue
Butt:	Black ostrich herl	Wing:	Strands of golden pheasant tippet, and the tip of a red golden pheasant body feather; over which are married strands of teal blue, lavender, black goose and golden pheasant tail; bronze mallard over
Body:	Rear ½: Flat silver tinsel, veiled on bottom with back to back small body feathers dyed blue chatterer blue Front ½: Black floss		
Rib:	Fine oval gold tinsel	Sides:	Black and white barred woodduck

Originated in 1990 by Mark Waslick of Middlebury, Vermont, for the Wenatchee River.

UMPQUA DREDGER

Tail:	Purple marabou and pearl crystal flash which extends from each side of the body		forward along the sides of the chenille body
Body:	Purple chenille	Hackle:	Purple, palmered over the body with a few extra turns taken as a collar
Sides:	Pearl crystal flash tied on the sides of the marabou tail and pulled	Head:	Silver bead chain eyes

The Dredger was designed in the late 1980s by Mike Mercer of the Fly Shop in Redding, California, for the summer-run on the North Umpqua River. It is not only effective on fresh-run summer fish, but seems also to move sulking fish that have become stale.

UMPQUA PERLY-BOU

Hook:	1/0 to 5/0		plumes over which are a several strands of pearl crystal flash
Tail:	Red hackle barbs		
Body:	Pearl Diamond Braid or pearl braided Mylar tubing, wrapped	Collar:	Long, soft, webby fluorescent orange hackle
Wing:	Three to five white marabou	Head:	Fluorescent red-orange

This is a large winter pattern from the North Umpqua and Joe Howell, of the Blue Heron Fly Shop. It is a good choice for fishing deep, fast, off-color water.

UMPQUA SPECIAL

Tail:	White hair or hackle barbs	Cheeks:	Jungle cock (optional - it appears that the title "Umpqua Special" is reserved for the fly when it is tied with jungle cock; without jungle cock it is simply called the "Umpqua")
Body:	Rear ⅓: Yellow wool or chenille, Front ⅔: Red wool or chenille		
Rib:	Flat or oval silver tinsel		
Wing:	White bucktail with a touch of red on the sides		
Collar:	Soft brown hackle		

Probably originated around 1935 by Vic O'Byrne, who operated one of two camps on the North Umpqua as concessions leased from the U.S. Forest Service. O'Byrne's camp was at Fish Rack Riffle, upriver of the better-known camp at Steamboat that was run by Major Mott. The Umpqua Special was a popular fly at that time and remains so today.

VAN LUVEN

Tail:	Red hackle barbs	Collar:	Brown hackle
Body:	Red yarn	Wing:	White bucktail
Rib:	Flat silver tinsel		

Introduced on the Rogue River in the 1920s by Harry Van Luven of Portland, Oregon, this fly was his attempt to develop a wet fly that incorporated the important elements of the highly-effective Royal Coachman, but was more durable. It is still a good fly, but perhaps is more popular in a version tied by "Polly" Rosborough who modified it with a fluorescent-red tail and hackle.

Tied by Farrow Allen

WAHLFLOWER

Hook:	Gold	Body:	Fluorescent green floss, lacquered
Tag:	Flat silver tinsel and fluorescent yellow floss (covering about half of the length of the hook shank)	Rib:	Oval silver tinsel
		Throat:	Golden pheasant crest
		Wing:	Gray squirrel tail dyed yellow
Tail:	Golden pheasant crest		

This is one of the better-known fly patterns, created in 1965 by Ralph Wahl of Bellingham, Washington. Wahl has been fly fishing for steelhead since the 1930s and is well-known for his magnificent black-and-white outdoor photographs. He is the author of several books including the recently-published *One Man's Steelhead Shangri-La*. The Wahlflower is a good fly for summer steelheading in low water.

Tied by Farrow Allen

WASHOUGAL OLIVE

Tag:	Fine oval gold tinsel (optional)	Rib:	Oval gold tinsel (optional)
Tail:	Golden-olive calftail	Throat:	Golden-olive calftail
Body:	Flat gold tinsel	Wing:	White calftail

The Washougal Olive was created in 1968 by Bill McMillan of Washougal, Washington. It is one of three flies called the Spring Simplicity Series that McMillan developed for the early, spooky steelhead that enter the Washougal in March, April and May. His intent was to create a fly that would blend naturally with the environment of the river yet be just bright enough to attract attention. This is the only one of the original three that became popular.

Tied by Bill McMillan

WEEKEND WARRIOR

Tail:	Red hackle barbs		tent style over the white hair
Body:	Silver tinsel yarn	Collar:	Fluorescent green hackle, the length of the wing and body
Underwing:	White calftail or skunk hair		
Overwing:	Two jungle cock feathers tied		

This fly was originally tied in 1971 by Eugene Sunday of Flushing, Michigan, as an attractor pattern for fishing high, dirty water on the Muskegon River. Sunday, a locally-known tier of classic Atlantic-salmon flies, also fishes the "Warrior" with a fluorescent-orange collar.

Tied by Eugene Sunday

Tied by Trey Combs

WINTER ORANGE

Tag:	Flat silver tinsel
Tail:	Orange hackle barbs
Body:	Fluorescent orange floss over a base of flat silver tinsel
Rib:	Flat silver tinsel
Wing (1):	Orange crystal flash (optional) over which is a plume of orange marabou to the end of the tail, over which is a shorter plume of orange marabou
Throat:	Orange marabou
Wing (2):	Red marabou
Collar:	Red or rose-red hackle
Head:	Fluorescent red

Developed by the author of *Steelhead Fly Fishing,* Trey Combs of Port Townsend, Washington, the Winter Orange fishes successfully for winter steelhead in both clear and cloudy water. It is one of a series of three patterns that includes the Winter Red and Winter Rose.

WINTER SHRIMP

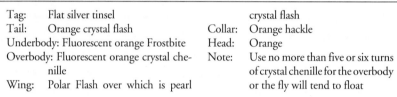

Tag:	Flat silver tinsel
Tail:	Orange crystal flash
Underbody:	Fluorescent orange Frostbite
Overbody:	Fluorescent orange crystal chenille
Wing:	Polar Flash over which is pearl crystal flash
Collar:	Orange hackle
Head:	Orange
Note:	Use no more than five or six turns of crystal chenille for the overbody or the fly will tend to float

Tied by John Shewey

During the 1986 season, John Shewey originated this "synthetic" version of the popular Polar Shrimp for winter steelheading in cold, off-colored water. It is best when fished in large sizes on heavy-wire hooks.

WINTER'S HOPE

Tied by Bill McMillan

Hook:	Heavy wire in sizes up to 6/0
Body:	Flat silver tinsel
Collar:	Turquoise blue hackle followed by purple, tied full
Wing:	Pair of yellow hackle tips on the outside of which are two fluorescent orange hackle tips
Topping:	Golden-olive calftail
Head:	Claret

This is a winter pattern that was developed over a two-year period by Bill McMillan of Washougal, Washington, in 1969 and 1970. The size and the color of this fly are intended to aggravate steelhead into striking by presenting a colorful, impressionistic form of familiar prey.

WINTERGREEN SPEY

Tied by Greg Scot Hunt

Tag:	Oval silver tinsel
Tail:	Golden pheasant crest dyed orange
Body:	Rear ½: Flat silver tinsel Front ½: Yellow-green fur
Rib:	Oval silver tinsel, over the dubbing only
Hackle:	Pheasant rump feather dyed yellow, palmered over the dubbing
Throat:	Pheasant rump feather dyed grass green, long
Wing:	Light green goose shoulder quill, tied tent style over the body
Cheeks:	Jungle cock set low
Head:	Yellow-green

Originated by Greg Scot Hunt of Redmond, Washington, for the Sauk River, this design utilizes ". . . a successful guide's most productive color combination." It's most effective for fishing at mid-day on bright winter days.

WOOLLY BUGGER

Hook:	Streamer hook about 4x long	Body:	Purple, olive or black chenille (these
Tail:	Black marabou and several op-		are three of the best colors)
	tional strands of crystal flash (color	Rib:	Copper or gold wire (optional)
	optional), both about 1½ times	Hackle:	Black, palmered forward
	the body length		

Here is a trout pattern that has proven to be very attractive to spawning steelhead. David Watterworth, a steelheader fom Lowell, Michigan, who dressed this pattern for us, suggests that steelhead take the Woolly Bugger so aggressively that setting the hook often isn't neccessary.

Tied by David Watterworth

WOOLLY BUGGER, CRYSTAL CHENILLE

Tail:	Olive marabou		forward
Body:	Olive crystal chenille	Head:	Olive
Hackle:	Olive dyed grizzly hackle, palmered		

This compact Woolly Bugger was tied by Keith Burkhart of the Valley Flyfisher in Salem, Oregon. His version is relatively short and almost nymph-like. Other tiers often employ marabou tails that are longer than the body, mixed with crystal hair or Flashabou. Some variations use full, webby hackles plus an additional neck hackle. There is virtually no end to the range of sizes, colors and shapes for the highly successful Woolly Buggers.

Tied by Keith Burkhart

WOOLY-WIFE

Tail:	White marabou plume over which	Hackle:	White, palmered over the chenille
	are silver Mylar strips, twice the		between the tinsel ribbing
	body length	Wing:	White crystal flash
Body:	White chenille	Head:	Red
Rib:	Silver Mylar tinsel		

Bob O'Brien of the Angler's Sport Shop and Canoe Company in Ann Arbor, Michigan, developed this fly in the form of a Woolly Bugger "... to mimic the colors and movement of the steelhead's open-water prey, the alewife." Dead drifted, stripped or twitched, it has proved effective for winter-run fish on most steelhead rivers that feed Lake Michigan. A variation called the Extra Stout, tied with black chenille, gold tinsel, crystal flash and grizzly hackle, has been been deadly on rivers in both Michigan and Alaska.

Tied by Bob O'Brien

YULTIDE

Tag:	Flat gold tinsel		stripped of barbs
Body:	Rear ⅓: Pink wool	Collar:	Teal flank feather
	Front ⅔: Light green dubbing	Wing:	Dee style strips of green goose
Rib:	Oval gold tinsel		shoulder
Hackle:	Pink, palmered with one side	Head:	Orange

The Yultide was originated in 1984 by veteran steelhead angler Michael Malloy of Everett, Washington. Malloy, who fishes two or three days a week throughout the year, says that this is one of his best flies during the winter for the Skykomish and the Pilchuck Rivers.

Tied by Mike Malloy

Egg Flies

Tied by Umpqua Feather Merchants

Tied by Fred Contaoi

Tied by Fran Verdoliva

BABINE SPECIAL

Tail: White marabou
Rear egg: Fluorescent orange chenille
Center collar: Red hackle
Front egg: Fluorescent orange chenille
Collar: White hackle

The Babine Special, one of the earliest egg patterns, originated in British Columbia and was named for the Babine River. It is often tied in other color combinations.

BATTLE EGG

Body: A strand of Glo-Bug yarn tied onto the hook shank facing back, pulled forward and tied down, and then back again, tied off and clipped to form a tuft at the tail. These steps are repeated as many times as needed until the desired egg size is achieved

Originated in 1984 by Fred Contaoi, from Redding, California, when he was guiding and tying flies fulltime.

BLUE GOO

Rear and front hackle: Dark blue Estaz chenille
Body: An egg of fluorescent orange chenille
Head: Fluorescent orange

Steelhead guide Fran Verdoliva chose this color combination because blue is an effective color for steelhead on New York's Salmon River. Early Double Egg Sperm flies were so successful tied with blue marabou that bait fisherman began making spawn bags with blue mesh. This fly represents the orange-egg and blue-mesh combination.

Tied by Jim Rusher

Tied by Fran Verdoliva

Tied by Gary Selig

ESTAZ EGG

Butt: Fluorescent rose yarn
Body: Teal blue Estaz chenille

This Egg pattern was tied by Jim Rusher immediately after he received his first shipment of Estaz chenille. Rusher is the owner of Whitaker's Sport Shop, the gathering spot for steelhead fly fishermen in Pulaski, New York, where he serves up Estaz Eggs in a variety of colors.

FOAM EGG

Tag: Silver tinsel
Tail: Blue marabou
Body: Orange foam egg
Head: Fluorescent red

Fran Verdoliva who introduced this fly describes it as deadly for steelhead in the fall, during salmon spawning, when many loose eggs drift "suspended . . . just off the bottom." Foam eggs in a variety of colors may be used to construct this pattern.

GLO-BRITE SINGLE EGG

Tail: Fluorescent red Antron yarn
Body: Fluorescent green Glo-Brite chenille
Eyes: Small silver bead chain (optional)
Head: Fluorescent red

Although it was first tied in 1985 by Gary Selig with standard fluorescent chenille, after Glo-Brite chenille became available, Selig has tied this pattern for New York's Salmon River exclusively with either orange or green Glo-Brite.

Tied by Kelvin McKay

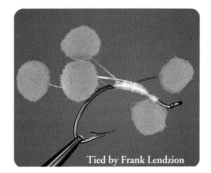

Tied by Frank Lendzion

Tied by Dick Stewart

BRIGHT ROE, ORANGE

Body: Fluorescent orange chenille
Rib: Flat silver tinsel
Wing: Fluorescent orange egg yarn and a very few strands of crystal flash
Head: Fluorescent orange

This popular pattern is tied in many colors for use in both Alaska and British Columbia. As with other yarn flies, the steelhead's teeth often tangle in the yarn's fibers, making the fly difficult to eject while providing the angler with valuable time to set the hook.

CLUSTER EGG

Hook: Caddis nymph
Thread: Flat white
Eggs: Pre-tied Glo-Bug eggs or novelty pom-poms, glued to stiff 15 or 20 pound monofilament

This radical-looking fly was sent to us by Frank Lendzion of the Wellston Inn in Wellston, Michigan. He "assembled" this variation using novelty store pom-poms which speeds up the tying process.

DOUBLE-EGG SPERM FLY

Tag: Gold tinsel
Tail: Golden pheasant crest
Body: Two balls of fluorescent orange chenille divided by flat gold tinsel
Collar: Fluorescent orange hackle
Wing: White marabou
Head: Fluorescent orange

This fly was originated by Dave Whitlock in the mid 1960s for salmon and steelhead in Alaska. It is sucessfully tied in many fluorescent colors, both weighted and unweighted. It is also known as the Two-Egg Sperm Fly.

Tied by Jeff Bowers

Tied by Bob Novak

Tied by Walt Grau

GLO-BUG

Thread: Extra heavy
Body: About four pieces Glo-Bug yarn in a single or combination of colors, tied on to the hook shank, pulled up and clipped to shape

The basic design of this fly is so simple that some fly dressers have difficulty referring to Glo-Bugs as flies. Regardless, Glo-Bugs originated in Anderson, California, at the Bug Shop and no one denies their ability to imitate natural trout or salmon eggs.

NOVAK BUBBLE EGG

Overbody sheath: Oregon cheese color Glo-Bug yarn
Underbody: Bright orange core of Glo-Bug yarn dubbed into a ball at the center of the hook
Note: Tie on the overbody yarn, dub the underbody core, pull the sheath forward over the core, and tie off

Bob Novak ties this pattern for Johnson's Pere Marquette Lodge in Baldwin, Michigan. Jim Johnson describes Novak's egg as "attractive and effective . . . this tied-down yarn tends to catch on everything sharp including the teeth of steelhead and salmon."

YARN EGG

Body: A short tuft of fluorescent orange Glo-Bug yarn in front of which is yellow Glo-Bug yarn spun around the hook
Collar: Fluorescent orange

This simple egg fly was provided by steelhead guide Walt Grau of Baldwin, Michigan. It was inspired by a spin fisherman who Grau observed in 1980 catching steelhead on a few strands of fluorescent yarn tied to a bare bait hook with spinning line. "Color variations are endless," says Grau, "but yellow with an orange center is hard to beat."

Shrimp

Tied by Bob Borden

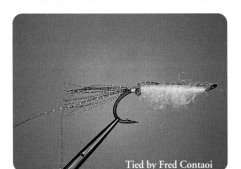

Tied by Fred Contaoi

Tied by Wayne Andersen

Tied by Barry Stokes

BORDEN'S PRAWN, HOT PINK

Eyes: Black bead chain eyes

Head-Rostrum: Fluorescent pink rabbit dubbing around the eyes to a position above the point of the hook.

Antennae: Golden pheasant tippet dyed fluorescent pink with center cut out, lacquered and formed to shape over which are about twelve strands of pink Krystal Flash tied in over and behind the bead chain eyes

Body: Strips of transversely cut fluorescent pink rabbit skin, palmered ¾ way up the hook

Back (1): Golden pheasant rump feather dyed fluorescent pink, tied flat on top

Body: Continue palmering rabbit strip to behind the eye of the hook

Back (2): Same as Back (1)

Originated in 1989 by Bob Borden of Monroe, Oregon. Borden introduced the transverse-cut fur strips which make this fly design unique. He ties this shrimp in various colors.

CRYSTAL SHRIMP

Antennae: Two long strands of black crystal flash tied over a shorter bunch of red crystal flash

Eyes: Fine silver bead chain eyes, tied on the underside of the hook

Body: Pink fur dubbing, picked out on bottom

Shellback: The red crystal flash used for the antennae, pulled over the top

Rib: A strand of pearl crystal flash, binding down the shellback

Head: Pink

This shrimp pattern was developed in the 1980s by Fred Contaoi, an active steelheader from Redding, California. Fred usually weights the body with lead wire and suggests fishing the Crystal Shrimp dead-drift in rivers, or retrieved in slack tidal water.

DARE DEVIL

Antennae: Long black bear hair and a few strands of pearl crystal flash

Eyes: Small green craft beads melted onto monofilament

Body: Black chenille

Hackle: Soft, natural black schlappen hackle over rear half of the body, trimmed under ribbed portion

Carapace: Black nylon raffia, a short portion extends over the antennae

Rib: Twisted strands of pearl crystal flash over rear 2/5 of body, binding down the raffia

Head: Red

This black prawn pattern was introduced by Wayne Andersen, a professional fly tier from Vancouver, British Columbia. The Dare Devil is easy to tie and an effective change-of-pace from the popular vivid-orange shrimp patterns.

EDGY POACHER

Antennae: Fluorescent orange hair

Eyes: Green glass beads melted onto monofilament

Carapace: Orange Edge Brite

Body: Fluorescent orange Estaz chenille

Hackle: Fluorescent orange, trimmed short on rear ½

Rib: Fluorescent orange thread

Head: Fluorescent red-orange

The Edgy Poacher was originated for winter fishing by Barry Stokes of Victoria, British Columbia, as a variation of the popular Squamish Poacher (which see). High visibility is achieved by utilizing a few of the brighter and flashier new fly-tying materials.

ESTUARY SHRIMP

Tail: Black calftail over pearl Flashabou
Body: Black dubbing
Rib: Pearl Flashabou
Collar: Sparse black hackle

Wing: Pearl Flashabou over which is black bucktail over which is shorter orange calftail
Head: Fluorescent red-orange

Designed by Les Johnson of San Francisco, for steelhead kelts which drop back downstream after spawning and feed heavily in the river estuaries before returning to the ocean. It has also proven effective on fresh fish upriver or as they pass through the tidal water before entering the river.

Tied by Farrow Allen

GENERAL PRACTITIONER, BLACK

Antennae: Black squirrel tail, length of body, half veiled by a small reddish golden pheasant breast feather
Rear ½ of body: Black mohair veiled by a single, narrow, black hen body feather
Front ½ of body: Black mohair continued, veiled by another 2 or 3 black hen body feathers extending nearly to the end of the first feather
Rib: Oval silver tinsel over entire body
Hackle: Palmered black saddle hackle, trimmed flat on the top so the hen feathers will lie flat

The Black General Practitioner was originated by Art Lingrin of British Columbia, for winter steelheading. This simplified version, Lingrin's latest, is a departure from the typically bright winter flies he suspected of often spooking shy fish in clear, shallow water.

Tied by Art Lingrin

GENERAL PRACTITIONER, CHARTREUSE

Tail: Divided chartreuse bucktail, over which is a tuft of chartreuse crystal flash
Body: Chartreuse wool
Rib: Oval gold tinsel
Hackle: Chartreuse, tapering towards the eye of the hook

Center carapace: Green-phase ringneck pheasant rump feather tied flat on top
Throat: Chartreuse hackle
Forward carapace: Green-phase ringneck pheasant rump feather

This is a steelhead version of Col. Esmund Drury's original General Practitioner used in fishing for Atlantic salmon. This fly was developed on the Skykomish River during the winter of 1985 by Washington fly tier Brad Beeson. It is most effective in sizes from 1/0 to 5/0, and is also tied in fluorescent-orange, pink or black.

Tied by Brad Beeson

GREAT LAKES SHRIMP

Tail: Tan sparkle yarn
Body: Cream sparkle yarn
Hackle: Cream, palmered forward over the body

Shellback: The balance of tan sparkle yarn pulled forward over the top
Eyes: Melted black monofilament
Head: Tan

This pattern was designed by Kelly Gallup and supplied by the Backcast Fly Shop in Benzonia, Michigan, where it continues to be a very popular fall and winter pattern. In clear water it appears natural - nearly transparent.

Tied by Backcast Fly Shop

Shrimp

HORNER'S SILVER SHRIMP

Tied by Wayne Orzel

Tail and back: Gray or tan deer body hair
Body: Large oval silver tinsel, built up
          over a floss base
Hackle: Soft grizzly hackle palmered over
          the body
Head: Black with painted white eye and
          black pupil

Developed in 1938 to be fished principally in tidewater at the mouth of a river, the Horner Shrimp was first used at the mouth of the Eel River in northern California and is one of the earliest-known shrimp patterns.

ORANGE SEAL

Tied by Alec Jackson

Body: Orange seal fur or substitute spun
         onto a loop of gold wire and dubbed
         onto the hook shank, full and well
         picked out
Collar: Soft orange hackle
Head: Fluorescent orange

This is a simple-yet-effective transluscent shrimp pattern designed by Alec Jackson of Kenmore, Washington. Primarily used for late-winter fishing in March and April on the Sauk and Skagit Rivers of Washington, where it is fished with good results.

SAUK RIVER SHRIMP

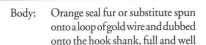
Tied by Alec Jackson

Tail: Orange bucktail
Body: Dyed red ostrich herl chenille,
         made by twisting the herl with fine
         oval silver tinsel, applied in four to
         six equal segments.
Hackle: At the completion of each seg-
         ment, several turns of orange hackle
         are made progressively tapering up
         towards the head where a final
         collar of orange is applied
Head: Fluorescent red-orange
Note: Effective variations may be tied in
         all-orange and all-black

Originated by Alec Jackson of Kenmore, Washington, and named for the river where he landed his first fly-caught steelhead. Jackson is the designer of the Alec Jackson series of Spey hooks that are distributed by his company, The Yorkshire Fly-Fisher, which is named after the Yorkshire district in northern England where he was born.

SQUAMISH POACHER

Tied by Joe Kambeitz

Antennae: Sparse orange bucktail
Eyes: Green glass eyes melted onto
         monofilament, slightly forward of
         the hook point
Body: Fluorescent orange chenille, fig-
         ure 8 around the eyes and built up
Hackle: Orange, full behind the glass eyes
         and palmered to the eye of the
         hook, trimmed flat across the top
         and around the abdomen
Carapace: Fluorescent orange surveyor's tape
         tied in over the hook eye, bound
         down over the abdomen, defining
         segments with the rib wire or
         thread, pulled forward and doubled
         over the thorax and tied off
Rib: Silver or copper wire or fluores-
         cent red-orange thread

This prawn fly was originated in 1974 by Joe Kambeitz, a conservationist and nature photographer from White Rock, British Columbia. It is a good producer during the winter, sinks well and is much brighter than most prawns. Kambeitz named it for one of his favorite rivers, and suggests fishing it "on a downstream swing along the bottom for best results."

SELECT BIBLIOGRAPHY

BOOKS

Alaska Flyfishers. 1983. *Fly patterns of Alaska.* Portland, Oregon: Frank Amato Publications

Boyle, Robert H. and Dave Whitlock, ed. 1978. *Second fly-tyer's almanac.* Philadelphia & New York: J.B. Lippincott

Combs, Trey. 1976. *Steelhead fly fishing and flies.* Portland, Oregon: Frank Amato Publications

————. 1991. *Steelhead fly fishing.* New York: Lyons & Burford

————. [1971] 1988. *The steelhead trout.* Portland, Oregon: Frank Amato Publications

Hellekson, Terry. 1981. *Popular fly patterns.* Salt Lake City: Gibbs M. Smith, Inc.

Hughes, Dave. [1986] 1989. *American fly tying manual.* 2d ed. Portland, Oregon: Frank Amato Publications

Inland Empire Fly Fishing Club. 1986. *Flies of the Northwest.* Portland, Oregon: Frank Amato Publications

Light, Tom & Neal Humphrey. 1979. *Steelhead fly tying manual.* Portland, Oregon: Frank Amato Publications

McMillan, Bill. 1987. *Dry line steelhead . . . and other subjects.* Portland, Oregon: Frank Amato Publications

Patrick, Roy. 1970. *Pacific northwest fly patterns.* Seattle: Patrick's Fly Shop

Richey, David. 1976. *Steelheading for everybody.* Harrisburg: Stackpole Books

————. 1979. *Great lakes steelhead flies.* Grawn, Michigan: Sportsman's Outdoor Enterprises, Inc.

PERIODICALS

American Angler. various dates 1990-1991. Intervale, NH: Northland Press

American Angler & Fly Tyer. various dates 1988-1990. Intervale, NH: Northland Press

American Fly Tyer. various dates 1986-1987. Intervale, NH: Northland Press

Fly Tyer. various dates 1978-1986. North Conway, NH: Fly Tyer, Inc.

Flyfishing the West. various dates 1978-1982. Portland, Oregon: Frank Amato Publications

Flyfishing. various dates 1982-1991. Portland, Oregon: Frank Amato Publications

INDEX TO FLY DRESSINGS

ABOUT THE AUTHORS

Dick Stewart (left) and Farrow Allen

Dick Stewart, has been tying flies since childhood and has been professionally involved in the fly-fishing industry for almost 20 years. He has authored or co-authored 5 fly-tying books including the best-selling *Universal Fly Tying Guide*. Dick's steelhead fishing has been in the Pacific northwest. Originally from Pennsylvania, Dick has settled in the White Mountains area of New Hampshire where he is Publisher of *American Angler* magazine.

Farrow Allen, moved from New York City to Vermont where for 12 years he owned a fly-fishing shop in the Burlington area. During this time he co-authored a book *Vermont Trout Streams*. A long time fly tier, Farrow has fished for steelhead in Oregon, Washington as well as in parts of the Great Lakes fishery. Currently he is associated with *American Angler* magazine and resides in New Hampshire.

ABOUT THIS BOOK

This is the second book in a series of five which cover the majority of recognized fly patterns in use in the United States and Canada. The series is entitled *Fishing Flies of North America* and the individual titles are as follows:

Flies for Atlantic Salmon
Flies for Steelhead
Flies for Bass & Panfish
Flies for Saltwater
Flies for Trout